THE LITTLE GUIDES

VEGETARIAN

W9-APJ-123

THE LITTLE GUIDES
VEGETARIAN

FOG CITY PRESS

Published by Fog City Press
814 Montgomery Street
San Francisco, CA 94133 USA
Reprinted in 2000 (twice), 2001, 2002

Copyright © 2000 Weldon Owen Pty Ltd

Chief Executive Officer: John Owen
President: Terry Newell
Publisher: Lynn Humphries
Managing Editor: Janine Flew
Art Director: Kylie Mulquin
Editorial Coordinator: Tracey Gibson
Production Manager: Martha Malic-Chavez
Business Manager: Emily Jahn
Vice President International Sales: Stuart Laurence
European Sales Director: Vanessa Mori

Project Editor: Lynn Cole
Designer: Leo Robba

All rights reserved. Unauthorized reproduction,
in any manner, is prohibited.

A catalog record for this book is available from
the Library of Congress, Washington, DC.

ISBN 1 875137 79 3

Color reproduction by Colourscan Co Pte Ltd
Printed by LeeFung-Asco Printers
Printed in China

A Weldon Owen Production

Contents

PART ONE
The Basics

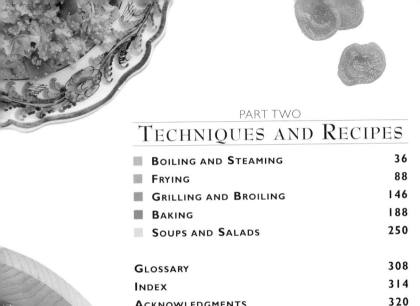

PART TWO

Techniques and Recipes

Introduction

Whether you are dedicated to the vegetarian way of eating or you just want to eat less meat for whatever reason, you will find the Little Guide to *Vegetarian* invaluable. It is designed to demonstrate the techniques used in cooking all manner of dishes and also to build your skills while you cook.

We show you in vivid photographs and explain in easy-to-follow step-by-step instructions how the professionals do things. It's all there at a glance, as if you were looking over the shoulder of a top chef. There are more than 70 recipes in this book and behind each one is many years of kitchen experience and testing by culinary experts.

Vegetarian is also the ultimate guide for anyone in need of practical information. Every important technique—from blanching, to cooking in a wok—is explained and demonstrated. The introductory chapters cover the basics of preparing vegetables, grains and legumes and selecting the equipment you will need to cook them. Later chapters focus on a particular cooking method, such as steaming, frying, grilling and baking, with appropriate recipes.

Each section builds on what you have already learned, with additional steps, techniques of special interest and tempting recipes. Each chapter is color-coded and valuable tips from the experts appear on virtually every page, along with stylish ideas for presentation and serving.

A glossary provides an overview of the ingredients used in the book and some of particular interest are dealt with in panels throughout the book, in conjunction with recipes in which they are used. The index provides quick reference to recipes that will quickly become family favorites.

To help you plan menus for every type of occasion, from casual to the most formal, the dishes in this book are beautifully photographed along with suggested accompaniments. Whether you are a novice or an experienced cook, you will find delicious recipes to help make your vegetarian meals as varied, interesting and appetizing as possible.

U.S. cup measures are used throughout this book. Slight adjustments may need to be made to quantities if Imperial or Metric cups are used.

Roasted Garlic Mashed Potatoes (see page 62).

PART ONE

THE BASICS

Professional chefs learn tricks and techniques that
make food preparation faster and easier. If you follow
their lead, you will be proud of your results and find
cooking more enjoyable.

Basic Techniques
for Preparing Vegetables

Never has our cornucopia overflowed with vegetables and grains in such a profusion of colors, textures and varieties. Thanks to improved methods of transportation and storage, today's home cooks have a glorious abundance to choose from at the market, regardless of season. The recipes in this book celebrate this incredible bounty.

On the following pages is all you need to know to prepare vegetables, grains and legumes. The techniques are simple, but fundamental: how to trim and shape any vegetable to preserve its flavor, cook it evenly and enhance its appearance; and how to turn raw grains and beans into savory dishes. You will use these skills over and over again in the chapters ahead and in all your cooking. Nothing is more elementary than an understanding of the differences between cubing, dicing and chopping, for example, or how to cut foods into julienne strips or on the bias. Each technique is clearly demonstrated and described, so you can prepare any recipe with confidence.

A large 6- or 8-in/15- or 20-cm chopping knife and a small 3- to 4-in/7.5- to 10-cm paring knife are essential tools for vegetable preparation. A chef's knife with a wide, slightly curved blade is a kitchen workhorse. Use it for chopping, slicing and mincing, and to transfer cut pieces from

BASIC TOOLS FOR PREPARING VEGETABLES

Basic vegetable preparation requires sharp
cutting tools, including large and small knives,
kitchen scissors and a swivel-bladed peeler.
A cup can be used when chopping herbs.

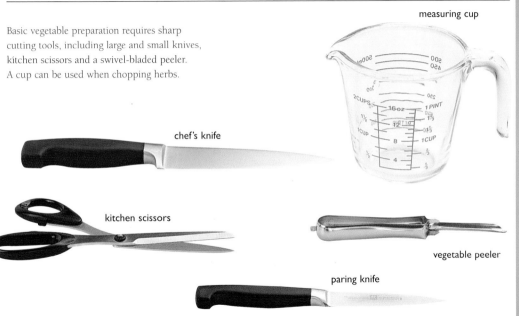

measuring cup

chef's knife

kitchen scissors

vegetable peeler

paring knife

work surface to cooking pot (its broad side serves as a scoop). A paring knife is like an extension of your hand—just the right size for peeling, removing bruised areas or slicing small shapes.

Although a substantial investment, quality knives will last a lifetime with good care. A good knife not only eases preparation, but is a form of insurance against kitchen accidents because it is easily sharpened and holds an edge longer. Sharp implements do their job with little effort; a dull blade can slip and cut you rather than the food. To prolong the life of any knife, always cut on a resilient surface such as wood or plastic; hard surfaces dull the edge. A vegetable peeler is another indispensable tool. Buy one that feels comfortable in the hand and will hold its edge (stainless steel is best).

For information on selecting and shopping for the vegetables used in this book, refer to the Glossary, which begins on page 308. Rice and grains are covered separately, on page 25, while legumes—including beans and lentils—appear on page 30.

The recipe for Steamed Vegetable Platter with Hollandaise Sauce appears on page 58.

Leave skin on until just before cooking to retain nutrients.

Slice off stem end, then remove skin with a paring knife, cutting spirally.

For smaller or larger pieces, vary the spacing of the cuts.

1. Peeling

Use a vegetable peeler for thin-skinned vegetables such as carrots, parsnips, radishes, asparagus and potatoes. Trim away the leafy tops and root ends, if any. Scrub the vegetables well, then peel off the skin with long, steady strokes.

2. Paring

Use a sharp paring knife for thick-skinned vegetables such as swedes and turnips. Slice off the stem end, then cut off skin in spirals (some flesh will be attached). Alternatively, cut off the ends and peel with a vegetable peeler, working from top to bottom all around.

3. Chopping Onions

Halve an onion from root to stem, then peel. Place one half, cut-side-down, on a work surface. Make a series of horizontal cuts parallel to the surface, almost to the root end. Then make vertical cuts from top to bottom. Finally, slice across, as shown, to create pieces. (Use this technique for similar vegetables.)

For greater stability, place flat side of vegetable (if any) on work surface.

The sharper the angle of the knife, the flatter the cut piece.

Garlic's papery skin will split and is then easy to peel away.

4. Slicing

To prevent the vegetable (here, celery) from slipping as you cut, anchor it firmly with your fingers. With a sharp knife, slice across with swift, clean cuts. Move your fingers back before the next cut or push the vegetable forward to keep slices even. Halve rounded vegetables horizontally first so one side is flat.

5. Bias Cutting

Place trimmed pieces (here, asparagus spears) on the work surface. Place a sharp chef's knife on the vegetable so that it slants away from you at an angle. Slice through, then continue slicing at regular intervals. The first piece will have an irregular shape. Vegetables are often cut in this way for use in stir-frying.

6. Peeling Garlic

Lay the widest part of the flat side of a chef's knife (near the handle) on the unpeeled clove of garlic. Pound the blade lightly with your fist to smash open the clove. Remove any peel and any bruised parts or green sprouting cores.

CHOPPING HERBS

1. Chopping with a Knife
Remove the leaves from the stems and place leaves in a pile on a cutting board. Using a chef's knife, hold the tip end down on the board with your fingers and chop with a rocking motion. Keep the herbs in a pile as you chop them into very fine pieces.

2. Chopping with Scissors
Strip off the leaves from fresh herbs and discard the stems. Place the leaves in a measuring cup or small bowl. With kitchen scissors, chop into small pieces.

If mincing more than one clove, chop them together.

7. Mincing Garlic
Peel the clove (see No. 6 on page 16). With a chef's knife and using a rocking motion of the blade, chop the clove until minced. If necessary, stop and push the garlic pieces into a pile once or twice.

Potatoes, eggplant (aubergines) and other rounded vegetables won't roll if a thin piece is first cut from one side to level them.

8. Cubing or Chopping
Make a series of lengthwise slices of the desired thickness. Stack the slices and make vertical cuts all the way through, of the same thickness as the first. Create cubes by cutting across perpendicularly into uniform squares. If desired, continue to chop into smaller pieces.

Dice are ⅛- to ¼-in/3- to 6-mm cubes.

9. Dicing

Cut lengthwise slices, as for cubing, but spaced closer together. Stack the slices and make vertical cuts spaced the same as the first slices. Create dice by cutting across perpendicularly.

For stability, remove the rounded outer side so the food sits flat on the work surface.

10. Cutting into Julienne Strips

Cut the vegetable into slices about 2 in/5 cm long and ¼ to ½ in/6 to 13 mm thick. Stack the slices and cut lengthwise again to make thin, matchlike sticks. Anchor the food (here, a carrot) with your fingers.

To retain the mushroom shape, trim only the bottom of the stem.

For halves, cut or pull out seed pod and stem; remove ribs with a knife.

The heat in a chili is concentrated in the oils in the ribs and seeds.

11. Trimming Stems

Use a sharp paring knife to trim away stems from vegetables such as mushrooms or artichokes. Trim the stems flush with the bottom of the vegetable or the underside of the mushroom cap; save for another use, if appropriate.

12. Coring and Trimming Bell Peppers (Capsicums)

Cut pepper into about 4 pieces, from ridge to ridge, with a sharp paring knife. Trim away any thick inner ribs plus the central core with stem and seeds. Each section is now clean and ready for further preparation.

13. Handling Chilies

Using a sharp paring knife, cut a chili in half. Cut away the ribs, seeds and stem. Protect your hands with gloves or a plastic bag to avoid the volatile oils that could burn your skin or eyes.

PEELING AND SEEDING TOMATOES

The skin will split in the water along the X mark.

1. Peeling Tomatoes

Cut an X in one end of a tomato and plunge the tomato into boiling water for about 30 seconds to loosen the skin. Drain and cool. Peel away the skin with a sharp paring knife.

Stubborn seeds can be pried out with your finger or the tip of a knife.

2. Seeding Tomatoes

Halve a peeled tomato across its midsection. Hold it upside down over a small bowl or the sink and squeeze and shake out the seeds.

Preparing and Cooking Rice and Grains

Appreciated the world over, grains play an important role in the diet. They add flavor and texture to meals, as well as important nutrients. When protein-rich foods are in short supply, grains are an economical and healthy way to extend them. And as grains are used so creatively in so many cuisines, the adventurous cook will find it easy to compile exciting menus that feature these ingredients.

Grains are the seed kernels of cereal plants that are members of the grass family. Most require some processing after harvesting to make them easier to cook and to digest. Rice, wild rice and barley, for example, must be husked; white rice and barley are also polished, an additional step. Groats, whole grains, or wheat berries (whole wheat kernels) are grains that are husked, but not polished or ground into flour, as corn is for cornmeal (maize flour) or polenta and wheat for couscous. Because they contain the complete kernel—bran, oil-rich germ and endosperm—grains in these forms take longer to cook and can turn rancid quickly if incorrectly stored.

The photo on page 25 illustrates the various grains used in this book; see page 30 for information on selecting and using grains and legumes.

Use a very fine-meshed sieve for rinsing grains, if necessary, then cook them in a heavy saucepan for the most uniform heat. When cooked, use a fork to fluff and separate the grains.

saucepan

fine-meshed sieve

1. Rinsing Wild Rice

Wild rice must be rinsed before cooking (basmati rice is often rinsed as well). Place the rice in a very fine-meshed sieve and rinse with running water to remove any particles or dust that remain after processing. Toss the rice to be sure the water reaches all of it. Alternatively, place the rice in a pan of warm water, stir, remove any pieces that float to the top, and carefully pour off the water.

fork

2. Boiling Grains

Bring a measured amount of water to a vigorous boil in a saucepan. Add seasoning, if called for, then the grain, such as the barley shown here. Stir once with a wooden spoon, cover and reduce heat to low.

3. Testing Doneness

At the end of the suggested cooking time, lift the cover; if all the liquid has been absorbed and the grain is tender, it is ready to eat. If mixture looks soupy, cook for a little longer. Depending on the grain, cooking time varies from 20–50 minutes.

4. Fluffing with a Fork

After cooking, let the grain sit, covered, for about 5 minutes. Remove the lid and fluff with a fork to separate the grains and make them easier to serve.

Be sure to use a large enough pan: during cooking, grains expand to up to four times their original size.

Don't have the heat too high or grains will burn and stick to the pan. Don't overcook grains.

Rice and couscous are two grains that require sitting time and fluffing.

couscous

pearl barley

quick-cooking
pearl barley

short-grain
brown rice

long-grain
brown rice

arborio rice

basmati rice

long-grain
white rice

short-grain
white rice

wild rice

cornmeal
(maize flour)

polenta

kasha (toasted
buckwheat groats)

bulgur (burghul
wheat)

wheat berries (whole
wheat kernels)

Preparing and Cooking Beans and Legumes

Dried beans, peas and lentils (*see photograph page 30*), are known collectively as legumes, a family of foods appreciated as a rich source of protein, vitamins and minerals. Black beans, red kidney beans and mottled pinto beans feature prominently in the cookery of Latin America and the southwestern United States; white cannellini beans are an Italian favorite; large and small white beans are common in robust casseroles, while lentils appear in hearty dishes in Europe, the Middle East and India. For advice on selecting and using the grains and legumes used in this book, turn to page 31.

With the exception of lentils, dried beans should be soaked before cooking. There are two ways to proceed: overnight soaking, as shown on page 28, or quick soaking.

Quick Soaking Cover the beans with a measured amount of water (use at least 3 times as much water as beans) and bring to a boil. Reduce heat and simmer, uncovered, for 2 minutes. Remove from the heat, cover and set aside for 1 hour. Drain off the soaking liquid and rinse, then cook as directed (boil dried red kidney beans for 10 minutes before cooking).

BASIC TOOLS FOR PREPARING AND COOKING BEANS AND LEGUMES

Rinse and sort beans in a wire sieve, then soak
and cook them in a large saucepan. A measuring
cup ensures exact additions, and spoons make it
easy to stir and serve.

saucepan

fine-meshed sieve

slotted spoon

measuring cup

spoon

Look for pebbles and scarred or broken beans.

If the room is warm, let the beans soak in the refrigerator, or quick soak for an hour (see page 26).

Add a little more more water if the beans are becoming dry before they are fully cooked.

1. Rinsing and Sorting

As a first step, place the beans in a fine-meshed sieve. Rinse under cold running water, tossing to wet all the beans. With your fingers, remove and discard any damaged beans or foreign material.

2. Overnight Soaking

Put the beans in a large pot. Fill the pot with enough cold water to cover the beans by about 2 in/5 cm or according to the recipe. Cover and set aside in a cool place for 8 hours or overnight. The beans will absorb almost all of the water and will expand and look plump.

3. Checking Cooked Beans

After soaking, drain beans in a colander and rinse well. Cook beans until they are soft or as directed in the recipe. Taste a bean, or pick one up and squeeze it with your thumb and index finger to see if it is tender. If it is still firm in the center, cook a little longer.

Selecting and Using Grains and Legumes

The following glossary provides information on the grains and legumes used in this book (*see pages 25 and 30 for photographs*). Store these ingredients in airtight containers. Beans, cornmeal (maize flour), couscous, lentils, pearl barley, polenta and white rice will keep for up to 1 year in a cool, dark, dry place. Grains that have their oil-rich germ and bran intact, including brown rice, bulgur (burghul) wheat, kasha (toasted buckwheat groats), wheat berries (whole wheat kernels) and wild rice, can turn rancid. Store them in a cool area, or refrigerate for up to 5 months.

GRAINS

Arborio rice Popular for the classic Italian risotto, this stubby, medium-grain white rice from northern Italy has a high starch content that dissolves into a creamy sauce when cooked and stirred in boiling liquid.

Basmati rice A staple of Indian cooking, but the nutty flavor of this fragrant, long-grain white rice suits any cuisine. Rinse, then cook as you would white rice, but with slightly less water.

Brown rice Only the husk is removed during the processing of short- and long-grain brown rice; the bran, endosperm and germ are left. The unpolished result is more tasty and nutritious than white rice, but requires longer cooking and has a shorter shelf life because the oil-rich germ encourages it to become rancid.

Bulgur (burghul) wheat When wheat berries (whole kernels) are steamed, dried and cracked, they become bulgur (burghul), a favorite Middle Eastern grain (ordinary cracked wheat isn't cooked and is

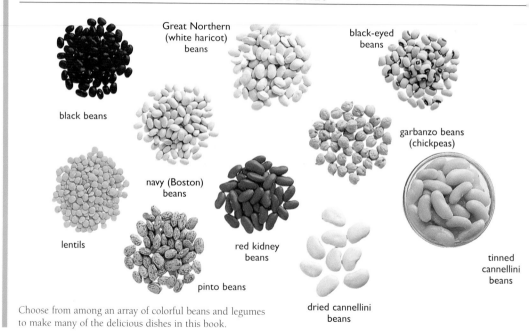

black beans

Great Northern
(white haricot)
beans

black-eyed
beans

navy (Boston)
beans

lentils

pinto beans

red kidney
beans

garbanzo beans
(chickpeas)

dried cannellini
beans

tinned
cannellini
beans

Choose from among an array of colorful beans and legumes
to make many of the delicious dishes in this book.

blander in taste). Highly nutritious, with a nutty flavor, this is ground both coarse and fine for use in salads, stuffings and pilafs.

Cornmeal (maize flour)

A key ingredient in American regional cooking, this sweet-tasting meal is finely ground from dried corn kernels that are typically white or yellow, but sometimes also blue in the American southwest. Use for breads, puddings and pancakes, and as a crunchy coating for fried foods.

Couscous These tiny pellets of semolina, the ground endosperm of durum wheat, are a type of pasta used throughout North Africa, especially in Morocco and Tunisia. A classic dish of the same name includes the grain along with meat, vegetables and seasonings.

Kasha (toasted buckwheat groats)

Nutty, crunchy toasted buckwheat kernels are sold in markets in two forms under the Russian name kasha: whole kernels, known as groats, and ground kernels, called grits. Use kasha in pilafs, casseroles and stuffings. Buckwheat groats, or whole kernels of buckwheat, are sometimes substituted for kasha in recipes. Because they are not toasted, they lack kasha's nutty flavor and crunch.

Pearl barley To make barley easier to cook and digest, it is polished, or pearled, up to six times. Pearl barley is mild and tender and is available in regular and quick-cooking forms for use in soups, pilafs and casseroles.

Polenta Italian cooks use this coarsely ground yellow cornmeal (maize flour) to make a type of porridge, which they enjoy in a number of ways: as a soft pudding, sliced then barbecued or pan-fried, or baked. Butter, cheese and various sauces are delicious accompaniments to polenta in any of its many forms.

Wheat berries (whole wheat kernels) These unprocessed whole kernels are highly nutritious—but require longer cooking—because they retain the bran, germ and endosperm. They make robust additions to cereals, stuffings, pilafs and breads.

White rice Both long- and short-grain white rice are polished to remove the tough outer hull. Because polishing also removes the bran and germ, white rice cooks more quickly than brown or wild rice, but is less nutritious unless the nutrients are restored during processing. Long-grain rice cooks firm and fluffy; short-grain rice, favored in Asia, tends to be stickier and more moist.

Wild rice Although referred to as a rice, wild rice is actually the seed of an aquatic grass native to North America. Dark brown, nutty and chewy, it was first harvested by Native Americans in Minnesota. Wild rice complements other grains, including white and brown rice.

LEGUMES

Black beans These small, flat dried beans have a meaty flavor and mealy texture. Also known as turtle beans, they are a favorite throughout Latin America and the Caribbean for soups, stews and in side dishes.

Cannellini beans Tender, meaty cannellini beans, a form of kidney bean, are prized in Italy—Tuscany in particular—for soups, casseroles and salads. Dried beans are preferred, but they also come precooked in tins. If using tinned beans, drain and rinse well before incorporating into recipes.

Black-eyed beans Popular in Africa and in the American south, these tiny dried beans with a black spot are earthy and meaty. They are mixed with rice in traditional dishes.

Garbanzo beans (chickpeas)
These earthy, round dried beans are most closely associated with the cuisines of the Middle East, North Africa and India and are probably best known as the base for hummus, a seasoned spread and dip.

Great Northern (white haricot) beans Large, white and plump, Great Northern beans have a mild flavor and can be substituted for cannellini beans in soups, casseroles and baked dishes.

Lentils Protein-rich lentils are small, disk-shaped dried seeds with a mild, nutty taste and soft texture. Native to Asia and a staple in the Middle East and India, they are available in red, yellow, pink and greenish-brown varieties. Lentils are superb additions to soups, salads and side dishes.

Navy (Boston) beans Small white navy beans are versatile enough to use in any recipe that calls for dried white beans. They are the bean of choice for many baked-bean dishes and also for many salads and soups.

Pinto beans Brown speckles on a tannish-pink skin distinguish this variety of dried bean. Its meaty flavor and mealy texture feature prominently in the soups and stews of Latin America, Mexico and the American southwest.

Red kidney beans In Europe, India, Australia and America, these meaty dried beans are familiar ingredients in salads, stews and soups. Dried red kidney beans should be boiled for 10 minutes after soaking and before cooking.

33

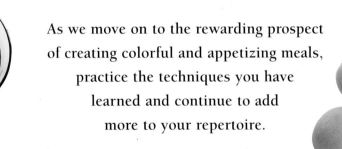

PART TWO

TECHNIQUES AND RECIPES

As we move on to the rewarding prospect
of creating colorful and appetizing meals,
practice the techniques you have
learned and continue to add
more to your repertoire.

BOILING AND STEAMING

Boiling and Steaming Vegetables and Grains

For most of us, childhood admonitions to "eat your vegetables" were heard all too often. Perhaps our reluctance to consume what should be delicious, naturally appealing food was prompted by plate after plate of vegetables overcooked to mush. We can't necessarily fault the cook: boiling vegetables beyond recognition was the rule for previous generations, rather than the exception. Fortunately, today we know better.

Properly executed, moist-heat methods such as boiling (and its variations, simmering and blanching) and the very gentle steaming are basic techniques that will cook vegetables, grains and legumes to the desired doneness with flavor and nutrition intact.

Simmering is recommended in some recipes when softer or more delicate vegetables need gentle cooking; long-cooking dried beans and grains are always simmered. Blanching incorporates a brief dip in boiling water to loosen skin (tomatoes), to set color and remove rawness (vegetables for crudités), or to partially cook (vegetables for stir-frying). A microwave oven (discussed on page 44) is also well suited to vegetables because it excels at moist-heat cooking and, along with steaming, minimizes the loss of water-soluble nutrients.

When boiling vegetables, be sure to use a pot large enough to allow small pieces to tumble freely and large pieces to be completely immersed in the cooking liquid (which needn't be limited to water; stocks can infuse vegetables with delicious flavor). Steaming locks in nutrients and is a good choice for quick-cooking vegetables such as green beans, zucchini (courgettes), or summer (baby) squash.

For steaming, some of the multipurpose pots with removable steamer inserts are a very useful investment if you enjoy steamed foods. One inexpensive option is a collapsible perforated steaming basket that sits inside a regular saucepan.

Test for doneness before the end of cooking time by probing one piece of vegetable with the tip of a knife or by taking a bite (be careful not to burn your mouth). For the most even result, pieces cooked together should be of similar

size, whether whole or cut up. When done, drain immediately to stop cooking.

Boiling and Steaming

Blanching is the first step for freezing or preparing crudités.

1. Blanching
Bring a large quantity of water to the boil. Add vegetables (here, sugar snap peas) and cook briefly. Just when the vegetables intensify in color and are barely crisp-tender (about 1 or 2 minutes) scoop them from the water with a sieve.

Rinsing also preserves the crisp texture of your vegetables.

2. Rinsing to Stop Cooking
As soon as the vegetables are blanched, rinse them under cold running water to stop the cooking and set their color. Toss, if necessary, so that all the vegetables come in contact with the water.

A simmer is when the bubbles form slowly and burst just below the surface of the water.

3. Boiling

Add water to a large pot and bring it to a rolling boil, then add vegetables (some recipes may ask you to place the vegetables in the pot first, then add water and heat). Reduce the heat to a slow simmer, if specified.

Always be careful to stand back as you pour, as the rising steam can burn.

4. Draining

As soon as the vegetables reach the desired stage of doneness, remove the pot from the heat and drain off the water by pouring the vegetables into a colander placed in the sink. Serve or use immediately, as the food will continue to cook from the retained heat.

Boiling and Steaming

Don't overload the steamer or the pieces will cook unevenly.

5. Steaming
Use a pot with a removable steamer insert or place a steamer basket in the pot. Add water to at least 1 in/2.5 cm below the steamer insert or just to the bottom of the steamer basket. Bring the water to a boil, place the prepared vegetables in the steamer, and cover. Adjust heat to maintain a steady boil.

Pay close attention to cooking times, as many vegetables finish cooking quickly.

6. Testing for Doneness
Begin checking for doneness a few minutes before the vegetables appear done. One of the best methods is to pierce a piece of vegetable with the pointed tip of a knife; when you feel that the knife slips easily into the food, the vegetable is done.

FREEZING HERBS

Freeze herbs at the peak of the season, when they are most plentiful and of the best quality. Herbs that freeze well include basil, burnet, chervil, chives, cilantro (fresh coriander), comfrey, sweet fennel, lovage, most mints (although some may blacken), parsley, savory and some thymes.

STEP 1

Blanching
Holding stems, dip herbs in boiling water and swish gently about. They are ready when the color brightens. This process takes only a few seconds.

STEP 2

Draining
Place the herbs, by the bunch, on clean paper towels to cool.

STEP 3

Preparing for Freezing
Prepare the herbs for freezing in any way that will be convenient for later use, by removing stems, chopping, or simply leaving them whole.

STEP 4

Wrapping
When air-cooled and dry, lay the herbs out in single layers on waxed paper, then roll up and label.

STEP 5

Freezing
Store in the freezer for use throughout the winter. Simply break off as much as you need each time from the frozen roll.

Steps for Microwaving Vegetables

Vegetables cook tender and crisp in minutes in a microwave oven. Because the cooking time is so brief, color, flavor and nutrients are preserved.

Use a heatproof glass or plastic dish labeled safe for the microwave. Remember the following hints for best results. Cut the vegetables in pieces of similar size. If cooking different vegetables in the same dish, be sure that they require the same amount of time. Thick stems, such as those of broccoli and asparagus, should point out to the sides of the dish. Be sure to pierce potatoes or any other whole vegetables cooked in their skins, or they might explode from a buildup of steam. To envelop vegetables in steam as they cook, cover the dish with a lid or with heavy plastic wrap (film). Most microwave recipes specify standing time in addition to cooking time, as microwaves continue to move through food even after it is removed from the oven. Stand the dish, still covered, for the amount of time indicated.

small glass bowl

spoon

44

Use heatproof dishes for microwave cooking. A small bowl is useful for blending herbed butter. A variety of spoons assist with measuring and mixing tasks.

microwave-safe dish

measuring spoons

wooden spoon

A small amount of water creates steam for rapid, even cooking.

STEP 1

Adding Water to Vegetables
Arrange vegetables, cut into pieces of similar size, in an even layer in a microwave-safe dish. Sprinkle with 1 or 2 tablespoons of water, depending on the type and amount of vegetable.

Boiling and Steaming

The vent helps to prevent steam burns to your hands when the covering is pulled away after cooking.

STEP 2

Covering Dish

If the dish doesn't have its own lid, cover it with a sheet of microwave-safe plastic wrap (film). Cover the dish tightly, stretching the wrap so it rests smoothly across the dish. Turn back one corner of the wrap to serve as a vent for steam to escape.

Turn the whole dish if the food cannot be stirred or rearranged.

STEP 3

Rearranging Vegetables

Halfway through cooking, carefully peel back the plastic wrap (film) and stir the vegetables to rearrange them so that they get equal exposure to the microwaves. If cooking big pieces, like broccoli stems, turn the ends that were facing the sides of the dish toward the center.

MAKING HERB BUTTER

STEP 1

Mashing Butter

Put the desired amount of softened butter or margarine into a bowl and add any finely chopped herb or combination of herbs. Use about 1 teaspoon of chopped herbs for every 2 oz/60 g of butter or margarine. With the back of a spoon, mash together herbs and softened butter or margarine.

STEP 2

Rolling Log

Scoop up the herb-butter mixture and place on a square of plastic wrap (film). Fold the plastic in half over the mixture; use it to shape the mixture into a log. Wrap securely and freeze or refrigerate until needed.

Herb butter makes an ideal topping for steamed, boiled or microwaved vegetables. It can be made ahead, wrapped in plastic wrap (film) and frozen ready for use.

Polenta alla Romana

Italian polenta, or coarsely ground cornmeal (maize flour), can be served as soft polenta or, as in this case, molded and chilled, then sliced, grilled, topped with cheese and served with a commercial or homemade salsa or tomato sauce. You might like to use leftover slices to make Grilled Polenta with Grilled-Tomato Sauce (*see recipe page 175*).

INGREDIENTS

3 cups/24 fl oz/750 ml water

½ teaspoon salt

6 oz/185 g polenta or coarse yellow cornmeal (maize flour)

1 cup/8 fl oz/250 ml cold water

3 oz/90 g grated Romano or Parmesan cheese

1 tablespoon olive oil or vegetable oil

Commercial tomato salsa or tomato sauce (optional), to serve

METHOD FOR MAKING POLENTA ALLA ROMANA

Preparation time 10 minutes
Cooling time 1 hour
Cooking time 40 minutes
Serves 8 as an accompaniment (16 slices)

Bring the 3 cups of water to the boil in a 2 qt/2 l saucepan with the salt. Combine the polenta or cornmeal with 1 cup cold water in a small mixing bowl; add 2 oz/60 g of the grated cheese. Slowly add the polenta mixture to the boiling water, stirring constantly. Cook and stir until the mixture returns to the boil. Reduce heat to very low. Cover and simmer, stirring occasionally, for 30–40 minutes, or until very thick. Pour the hot mixture into a greased loaf tin 8 x 4 x 2 in/20 x 10 x 5 cm. Cool for 1 hour. Cover and chill for several hours, or overnight, until firm.

Preheat the grill at serving time. Remove polenta from tin and cut into 16 slices, each about ½ in/1 cm thick. Place slices in a single layer on the greased rack of a grill pan. Brush lightly with oil. Sprinkle with the remaining 1 oz/30 g grated cheese. Grill 4 in/ 10 cm from the heat for 3–5 minutes, or until cheese is light golden brown. Serve plain or, if desired, with salsa or tomato sauce.

Golden slices of cooked polenta flavored with pungent Romano cheese develop a crisp surface when barbecued or grilled, while the centers stay soft and creamy.

STEP 1

Adding Polenta to Water
Slowly add the polenta mixture to the boiling water, stirring constantly to avoid lumps. Keep stirring until the mixture returns to the boil. The mixture will thicken quickly but needs to be cooked over low heat for about 30–40 minutes to eliminate the raw taste.

STEP 2

Shaping Polenta
After about 35 minutes of cooking and stirring, the polenta will be very thick. With a spatula, transfer the hot mixture to a greased loaf tin and set aside to cool. Refrigerate, covered, until firm enough to slice.

STEP 3

Cutting Polenta
To prepare for serving, first remove the chilled, firm polenta from the loaf tin and invert onto a cutting board. With a long, sharp knife, cut into 16 equal slices and proceed as directed in the recipe.

About Polenta

Polenta is a ground cornmeal that comes in three degrees of fineness, fine, medium and coarse. You may find the coarse-grained meal easier to cook without lumps, which must be avoided at all costs as they spoil the texture. Because polenta is made from different types of corn, it's worth experimenting with different brands to find the one you like best. Experiment, too, with the quantity of water you use. You may find that you prefer the softer texture achieved with more water. Try, also, some of the instant polentas, but many people find these preparations too heavy.

To cook Bring 5 cups/40 fl oz/1.25 l salted water to the boil in a large pot. Pour in 8 oz/250 g polenta, lower the heat and stir vigorously, some recipes say in one direction only, until it forms a kind of porridge. There should be no lumps. Continue to cook, stirring, for 30–40 minutes, or until the polenta starts to leave the sides of the pot clean and there is no raw taste. Spread in a slab in a greased loaf tin or on a wet pastry board and serve, cut into slices, with cheese. Leftover polenta is delicious brushed with oil and grilled or barbecued as a high-carbohydrate accompaniment in place of potatoes.

To store Buy polenta in small quantities and use within a few months. Store in an airtight jar in a cool place to avoid spoiling.

Artichokes with Dijon–Herb Mayonnaise

If you are cutting down on cholesterol, this delicious herb mayonnaise,
using frozen egg substitute, is for you, but use raw eggs if you prefer.
It also makes an excellent dip for asparagus.

INGREDIENTS

DIJON–HERB MAYONNAISE

¼ cup/2 fl oz/60 ml refrigerated
or frozen egg substitute, thawed,
or 1 large egg

4 teaspoons fresh lemon juice

1 tablespoon finely chopped
fresh basil or 1 teaspoon dried
basil, crushed

1 tablespoon finely chopped fresh
thyme or 1 teaspoon dried
thyme, crushed

1 tablespoon Dijon mustard

½ teaspoon salt

1 cup/8 fl oz/250 ml olive oil
or salad oil

ARTICHOKES OR ASPARAGUS

4 medium to large globe
artichokes or 1 lb/500 g
asparagus

Fresh lemon juice

Steamed globe artichokes make a delicious hot or cold first course for entertaining. They are easy to serve—guests simply dip the tender leaf bases in the delicate mustard-infused mayonnaise.

Boiling and Steaming

Preparation time 15 minutes
Cooking time 20 to 25 minutes
Makes 4 servings as an accompaniment or first course

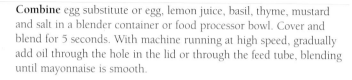

Combine egg substitute or egg, lemon juice, basil, thyme, mustard and salt in a blender container or food processor bowl. Cover and blend for 5 seconds. With machine running at high speed, gradually add oil through the hole in the lid or through the feed tube, blending until mayonnaise is smooth.

Trim artichoke stems and remove loose outer leaves. Cut off 1 in/ 2.5 cm from tops; snip off sharp leaf tips. Brush cut surfaces with lemon juice. Place in a steamer basket over water in a large saucepan. Bring to the boil; reduce heat to simmering. Cover and steam for 20–25 minutes, or until a leaf pulls out easily. (Or, for asparagus, wash; scrape off scales. Break off woody bases where spears snap easily. Place in a steamer basket over boiling water in a covered saucepan. Steam for 5–8 minutes, or until crisp-tender.) Remove from steamer basket.

Serve artichokes, hot or chilled, with mayonnaise. (For asparagus, arrange spears on 4 serving plates; spoon over some of the mayonnaise.) Any leftover mayonnaise can be stored in an airtight container in the refrigerator for up to 1 week.

STEP 1

Trimming Stems

Place an artichoke on its side on a cutting board. With a sharp knife, trim off the stem flush with the bottom of the artichoke.

STEP 2

Trimming Tops

Snap off any small, loose or discolored outer leaves. With a sharp knife, slice off about 1 in/ 2.5 cm of the top in an even piece.

STEP 3

Trimming Leaf Tips

Cut off the sharp leaf tips with kitchen scissors. Cut them straight across, or at an angle for a more decorative effect.

Vegetable Stock

Use this full-bodied vegetable stock in place of any meat or fish stock.
Purchased vegetable stock can be used in place of homemade
when time is short.

INGREDIENTS

2 tablespoons extra-virgin
olive oil

5 oz/155 g diced carrot

4 oz/125 g diced celery

2 oz/60 g sliced leeks

1 small clove garlic

1 small red (Spanish) onion, cut
in half

12 oz/375 g fresh white
mushrooms, cut in halves

8 cups/64 fl oz/2 l cold water

1 small plum (Roma) tomato

½ teaspoon fresh thyme leaves
or ¼ teaspoon dried thyme

½ teaspoon fresh marjoram
leaves or ¼ teaspoon dried
marjoram

4 fresh parsley sprigs

Salt and freshly ground pepper

Warm olive oil in a saucepan over low heat. Add carrot, celery and leek and cook for 3–4 minutes, or until leeks are slightly translucent.

Add garlic, onion and mushrooms and cook for about 2 minutes, or until onion is slightly translucent.

Pour in water and bring to the boil over high heat. Using a large spoon, skim any scum from the surface, if necessary. Add tomato, thyme, marjoram and parsley. Reuce heat and simmer, uncovered, about 1 hour, or until the flavors are blended.

Strain stock through a fine mesh sieve lined with cheesecloth (muslin) into one or more clean containers. Use immediately, or cover and refrigerate for up to

3 days, or freeze for up to 1 month. Season to taste with salt and pepper when using.

Preparation time 15 minutes
Cooking time 1¼ hours
Makes about 5 cups/40 fl oz/1.25 l

Steamed Vegetable Platter with Hollandaise Sauce

This easy version of the classic hollandaise is delicious served with cooked vegetables, but it also goes well with eggs. A double boiler makes it easier to control the heat when cooking the egg yolks.

INGREDIENTS

HOLLANDAISE SAUCE

3 egg yolks, beaten

1 tablespoon water

1 tablespoon fresh lemon juice

Pinch salt

Pinch white pepper

4 oz/125 g margarine or butter, at room temperature, cut into thirds

VEGETABLES

Vegetable stock or water

2 teaspoons dried basil, sage, or oregano, crushed

1 to 1½ lb/500 to 750 g cut-up mixed fresh vegetables, such as zucchini (courgettes), eggplant (aubergine), jícama (yam bean), asparagus, bell peppers (capsicums), carrots, parsnips, Brussels sprouts, turnips

A smooth, buttery hollandaise sauce lends elegance to a platter of simple steamed vegetables.

Preparation time 15 minutes
Cooking time 8 to 15 minutes
Makes 4 to 6 servings as an
accompaniment or first course

For hollandaise sauce, whisk egg
yolks in the top of a double
boiler with water, lemon juice,
salt and pepper. Add 1 piece of
the margarine or butter. Place
over boiling water (upper pan
should not touch water). Cook,

stirring rapidly, until margarine
or butter melts and sauce begins
to thicken. Stirring constantly,
add the remaining margarine or
butter, a piece at a time. Cook,
stirring, for 1–2 minutes, or
until sauce thickens. Remove
from heat immediately. If the
sauce is too thick or has curdled,
immediately beat in 1–2 tablespoons hot water. Keep warm
over hot water.

For vegetables, fill a 4-qt/4-l
saucepan with 1 in/2.5 cm of
vegetable stock or water; stir in
dried herbs and bring to the
boil. Arrange selected cut-up
vegetables in a steamer basket
and place in saucepan. Cover
and steam until vegetables are

tender. Allow 3–4 minutes for
¼-in/6-mm-thick zucchini
(courgette) slices, ¾-in/2-cm
eggplant (aubergine) cubes,
½-in/1-cm jícama (yam bean)
cubes and asparagus spears;
5–6 minutes for bell pepper
(capsicum) strips; 8–10 minutes
for ¼-in/6-mm-thick carrot or
parsnip slices, halved Brussels
sprouts, or ½-in/1-cm turnip
cubes. Remove vegetables and
arrange on a platter. Spoon
hollandaise over vegetables or
serve in a separate bowl for
dipping the vegetables.

Boiling and Steaming

STEP I

Adding Margarine or Butter

In the top of a double boiler, stir the margarine or butter into the sauce one piece at a time, whisking constantly. Don't add the next piece until the previous one is melted and fully incorporated.

STEP 2

Consistency of Sauce

After adding the margarine or butter, cook and stir the sauce briefly, until satiny smooth and thickened. It is done when it falls in a medium-thick ribbon from a spoon lifted above the saucepan.

Roasted Garlic Mashed Potatoes

How can you improve on comforting mashed potatoes? Flavor them with mellow roasted garlic and sweet-pungent green (spring) onions, blended into a potato mixture enriched with cream and margarine or butter.

INGREDIENTS

6 cloves garlic, unpeeled

1 tablespoon cooking oil

1½ lb/750 g potatoes

2 tablespoons chopped green (spring) onions or fresh chives

2 oz/60 g margarine or butter

½ cup/4 fl oz/125 ml light (single) cream or milk

¼ teaspoon salt

⅛ teaspoon pepper

Roasting tames garlic's bite and gives it a toasted, almost sweet flavor that permeates these creamy mashed potatoes.

Preparation time 15 minutes
Cooking time 25 to 30 minutes
Makes 6 servings as an accompaniment

Place unpeeled garlic in a baking dish or pie plate; pour oil over garlic and toss to coat evenly. Cover tightly with foil. Bake in a preheated 400°F/200°C/Gas Mark 5 oven for about 25 minutes, or until garlic is tender when pierced. Remove garlic from oven; cool slightly.

Meanwhile, peel and quarter potatoes. Cook, covered, in boiling salted water to cover for 20–30 minutes, or until tender. Drain potatoes.

Squeeze garlic to extract the pulp. In a large mixing bowl combine the potatoes, garlic, spring onion or chives, margarine or butter, light cream or milk, salt and pepper. Beat with an electric mixer on medium speed to mash lightly, or beat well with a fork. Serve warm.

STEP 1

Preparing Garlic

Place the unpeeled garlic cloves in a heatproof glass baking dish. Drizzle with 1 tablespoon of oil, then toss the cloves to coat them in the oil.

STEP 2

Peeling Garlic

Hold the top end of a slightly cooled clove between thumb and index finger. Squeeze the garlic to force the clove out of the papery skin through the root end. Discard skins.

STEP 3

Mixing Potatoes

Place all the ingredients in a mixing bowl, including the roasted garlic pulp. Mash lightly with an electric mixer (do not overmix or potatoes will be sticky), or use a potato masher or a fork.

Two-Mushroom Risotto

Dried mushrooms have a rustic intensity and depth of flavor that give a boost to mild fresh mushrooms. If prepared in the traditional way with Italian Arborio rice, this dish will absorb the greater amount of liquid. Alternatively, make it as a traditional pilaf in a covered pan, using short-grain rice and a smaller amount of stock.

INGREDIENTS

½ oz/15 g broken-up dried mushrooms such as porcini, cèpes or shiitakes

2¼ to 4 cups/18 to 32 fl oz/ 560 ml to 1 l vegetable stock

3 tablespoons margarine or butter

5 oz/155 g chopped mushrooms

4 oz/125 g chopped onion

1 clove garlic, minced

1 teaspoon dried basil, sage or oregano, crushed

¼ teaspoon pepper

7 oz/220 g Arborio rice or short-grain rice

1½ oz/45 g grated Parmesan cheese

A blend of fresh and dried mushrooms flavors this earthy risotto.

METHOD FOR MAKING TWO-MUSHROOM RISOTTO

Preparation time 25 minutes
Standing time 30 minutes
Cooking time 25 to 30 minutes
Makes 6 servings as an
accompaniment

Place dried mushrooms in a
small bowl; pour boiling water
over to cover. Let stand for 30
minutes. Drain, reserving

soaking liquid. If liquid is gritty,
strain it through a sieve lined
with cheesecloth (muslin), or
through a coffee filter.

Bring vegetable stock and
soaking liquid to the boil in a
medium saucepan; reduce heat
to low. Meanwhile, in a large
saucepan melt margarine or
butter. Cook and stir drained
dried and chopped fresh
mushrooms, onion, garlic, basil,
sage or oregano and pepper for
about 5 minutes, or until tender.
Add rice; cook and stir until
coated with margarine or butter.

If using Arborio rice, add 1 cup/
8 fl oz/250 ml of the hot stock
mixture; cook over medium

heat, stirring constantly, until
nearly all liquid is absorbed.
Add more stock, just enough to
barely cover rice; cook, stirring
constantly, until stock is nearly
absorbed. Repeat adding stock
and cooking it down until rice is
tender and nearly all liquid is
absorbed, about 18–25 minutes.
(For short-grain rice, after
coating with margarine or butter,
add stock mixture, all at once;
bring to the boil. Reduce heat
and simmer, covered, for about
15 minutes, or until rice is
tender and liquid is absorbed.
Do not stir.) Stir in Parmesan
cheese and serve.

STEPS FOR MAKING TWO-MUSHROOM RISOTTO

STEP 1

Soaking Mushrooms

Place the dried mushrooms in a small bowl and cover with boiling water. Let stand for 30 minutes. Drain and reserve the liquid.

STEP 2

Coating Rice

After the mushrooms and other ingredients have cooked in the margarine or butter, stir in the rice. Stir with a wooden spoon until the rice is thoroughly coated with margarine or butter.

STEP 3

Adding Stock

Have the stock and reserved mushroom soaking liquid simmering in a saucepan. Add the hot liquid to the rice mixture ladle by ladle, stirring constantly. Be sure each ladle of liquid is fully absorbed before adding the next.

Layered Bean Dip

Save time in the preparation of this popular Mexican dip by cooking the beans one day ahead. Let them cool to room temperature, then cover and chill them overnight.

INGREDIENTS

5 oz/155 g dried black or red kidney beans

8 cups/64 fl oz/2 l cold water

1 onion, chopped

½ teaspoon salt

½ teaspoon ground cumin

2 cloves garlic, minced

¼ teaspoon pepper

6 oz/185 g shredded lettuce

2½ oz/75 g sliced pitted black olives

3 ripe avocados, peeled and pitted

⅔ cup/5 fl oz/160 ml bottled salsa

4 oz/125 g shredded Cheddar or mild melting cheese

Fresh cilantro (coriander/Chinese parsley) or parsley sprigs

Corn chips

The cool refreshment of an icy Margarita provides a soothing contrast to a spicy dip constructed in layers with beans, avocado and salsa.

METHOD FOR MAKING LAYERED BEAN DIP

Preparation time 20 minutes
Standing time 1 hour to overnight
Cooking time 1 to 1½ hours
Makes 8 to 10 servings as a
first course

Rinse beans. Combine the uncooked beans and 4 cups/ 32 fl oz/1 l cold water in a 2-qt/2-l saucepan. Bring to the boil; reduce heat. Simmer for 2 minutes; remove from heat. Cover and let stand for 1 hour. (Or omit simmering and soak beans in 4 cups/32 fl oz/1 l cold water in a covered 2-qt/2-l saucepan overnight.) Drain and rinse beans. (If using red kidney beans, boil 10 minutes in water to cover, then drain again.)

Return beans to pan with 4 cups/32 fl oz/1 l fresh water. Add onion. Bring to the boil; reduce heat. Cover and simmer, stirring occasionally, for 1–1½ hours, or until beans are tender.

Drain beans, if necessary; place in a blender container or food processor bowl. Add salt, cumin, garlic and pepper. Cover and blend or process until nearly smooth. Cool bean mixture.

Line a platter with shredded lettuce. Spread or spoon bean mixture onto lettuce. Sprinkle olives over beans. Mash the avocados; stir in 2 tablespoons of the salsa and spread mixture over olives. Spoon on remaining salsa. Sprinkle with cheese. Garnish with coriander or parsley. Serve with corn chips.

STEPS FOR MASHING AVOCADOS

STEP 1

Cutting Avocados

With a sharp paring knife, divide an avocado into 4 sections by cutting from top to bottom, but working the knife around the stone.

STEP 2

Removing the Stone

Twist each pair of sections slightly to loosen them from the stone. Remove 3 of the 4 quarters with your fingers. Pull off the stone from the remaining section. Peel all 4 sections.

STEP 3

Mashing Avocados

Place peeled, pitted avocado quarters in a glass pie plate. With the back of a fork, mash the pieces until combined into a fairly smooth mass, but leave enough lumps to give a pleasant texture.

Spinach Gnocchi in Gorgonzola Cream Sauce

You're sure to find these little dumplings on trattoria tables in northern Italy during winter. For the lightest gnocchi, use yellow-fleshed potatoes, such as Yukon Gold or Finnish Yellow; white-fleshed varieties produce denser, but no less delicious, results.

INGREDIENTS

SPINACH GNOCCHI

1 1/4 lb/625 g fresh spinach, stems removed, or 1 package (10 oz/315 g) thawed frozen leaf spinach

26 oz/815 g yellow-fleshed potatoes, unpeeled, cut into large pieces

12 1/2 oz/390 g all-purpose (plain) flour, plus 2 1/2 oz/75 g flour for dusting

1 extra large egg

GORGONZOLA SAUCE

2 cups/16 fl oz/500 ml heavy (double) cream

2 oz/60 g sweet Gorgonzola cheese, crumbled

1/4 cup/2 fl oz/60 ml fruity Italian white wine

1 teaspoon Cognac or other brandy (optional)

Salt and freshly ground pepper

Freshly grated nutmeg

For a warming and satisfying first course, serve these meltingly tender little gnocchi with a tangy Gorgonzola sauce.

Boiling and Steaming

Preparation time 15 minutes
Cooking time 20 minutes
Makes 8 servings as a first course,
4 as a main course

Place spinach, if using fresh, on a steamer rack over boiling water (not touching). Cover and steam for 3–4 minutes, or until wilted and tender. Transfer rack to the sink so spinach can drain and cool.

Using your hands, gather the cooled spinach (or thawed frozen spinach, if using that) into a ball; squeeze out any excess moisture. Purée spinach in a food processor until smooth. Transfer onto paper towels and squeeze out remaining moisture. Set aside.

Steam potatoes for 8–10 minutes, or until tender. Peel while still hot and pass through a ricer to make a broad, low mound on a clean work surface. Sprinkle on the main portion of flour and quickly and gently "fluff" the flour and potato together with your fingertips.

Place spinach purée on top and, using a fork or your fingertips, work it into the dough. Place the egg on top and lightly mix in. Press the dough together and knead until smooth.

Scrape the work surface clean and sprinkle with flour. Divide dough into 6 equal portions and cover 5 with a kitchen towel to stop them drying out. Form remainder into a log about ¾ in/2 cm in diameter.

Cut log crosswise into pieces ¾ in/2 cm wide. If pieces are sticky, dust lightly with more flour. Repeat with remaining 5 portions.

Fill a deep saucepan three-fourths full with salted water and bring to a rolling boil. Add gnocchi, all at once, separating gently with a spoon. Boil for 12–15 minutes, or until just cooked through.

Meanwhile, for the sauce, boil the cream in a frying pan over high heat for about 4 minutes, or until slightly thickened. Stir in cheese and reduce heat. Add wine and simmer for 1 minute; add brandy and seasonings.

Drain gnocchi and add to the sauce, tossing to coat. Serve at once.

Moroccan Vegetable Couscous

Couscous, a beadlike pasta made from ground semolina, has been a staple in North Africa for years and is now becoming popular here. It cooks in just five minutes and you'll find it in the rice and pasta section at the grocery or supermarket.

INGREDIENTS

1 tablespoon olive oil

2 oz/60 g chopped onion

2½ oz/75 g chopped red or green bell pepper (capsicum)

1¼ oz/40 g chopped peeled carrot

1¼ oz/40 g chopped zucchini (courgette)

1 cup/8 fl oz/250 ml vegetable stock

5 oz/155 g shredded cabbage

6 oz/185 g chopped tomatoes (2 medium)

1 tablespoon finely chopped fresh cilantro (coriander/ Chinese parsley) or parsley

¼ teaspoon salt

¼ teaspoon ground cardamom

¼ teaspoon caraway seeds

⅛ teaspoon ground turmeric

4 oz/125 g couscous

Tiny pellets of couscous, a Moroccan pasta, make a delicious base for a medley of colorful vegetables and exotic spices.

Preparation time 15 minutes
Cooking time 20 minutes
Makes 6 servings as an accompaniment

Heat olive oil in a medium saucepan. Cook onion,
pepper, carrot and zucchini in the hot oil for 5 minutes.
Stir in stock, cabbage, tomato, cilantro or parsley, salt,
cardamom, caraway seeds and turmeric. Bring to the boil;
reduce heat. Cover and simmer for 10 minutes. Uncover;
stir in couscous. Remove from heat and let stand,
covered, for 5 minutes. Uncover and fluff up the grains
with a fork.

Ratatouille-Style Vegetable Stew

True French ratatouille is a hearty vegetable stew of eggplant (aubergine), tomatoes, summer (baby) squash, onions and green bell peppers (capsicums), but the choice can be unlimited, as evidenced in this eclectic version.

1 tablespoon olive oil

1 medium onion, sliced and separated into rings

2 cloves garlic, minced

1 lb/500 g cut-up mixed fresh vegetables, such as sliced carrots; diced peeled parsnips, potatoes, kohlrabi, turnip or swedes; sliced celery; and/or julienne strips of red or green bell pepper (capsicum) or sliced zucchini (courgettes)

1 medium eggplant (aubergine), peeled and cubed

1½ cups/12 fl oz/375 ml vegetable stock

2 large tomatoes, peeled (if desired) and chopped

1 tablespoon finely chopped fresh basil or 1 teaspoon dried basil, crushed

1 tablespoon finely chopped fresh rosemary or 1 teaspoon dried rosemary, crushed

1 bay leaf

1 teaspoon salt

¼ teaspoon pepper

The bountiful harvest of a Mediterranean kitchen garden is combined in this glorious vegetable dish.

Boiling and Steaming

Preparation time 30 minutes
Cooking time 40 minutes
Makes 8 servings as an accompaniment

Heat olive oil in a 4-qt/4-l saucepan; cook onion and garlic in hot oil, stirring, for 5 minutes. Add your choice of carrots, parsnips, potatoes, kohlrabi, turnip, swedes and/or celery. Add eggplant, stock, tomatoes, basil, rosemary, bay leaf, salt and pepper. Bring to the boil; reduce heat. Cover and simmer, stirring occasionally, for 20 minutes. If using, add bell pepper and/or zucchini. Cover and simmer for 10 minutes more. Remove and discard bay leaf.

Oat and Barley Cereal

Grains aren't reserved just for dinner. Here nutrient-and-fiber-packed oats and barley combine in a fruit-studded, stick-to-the ribs cereal. If you want to make this the night before, reheat it the next day in a saucepan with 2 tablespoons of water. Quick-cooking barley and barley flakes are available from well-stocked groceries and supermarkets.

INGREDIENTS

2½ cups/20 fl oz/625 ml water

1 cup/8 fl oz/250 ml milk

3 oz/90 g regular rolled oats

3 oz/90 g quick-cooking barley or barley flakes

3 tablespoons packed brown sugar

¾ teaspoon ground cinnamon

⅛ teaspoon salt

3 oz/90 g chopped dried fruit, such as dates, apricots, apples, pears, prunes or raisins

Milk to serve (optional)

Two nutritious grains are cooked with dried fruit, brown sugar and cinnamon for a sustaining and satisfying breakfast dish.

METHOD FOR MAKING OAT AND BARLEY CEREAL

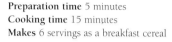

Preparation time 5 minutes
Cooking time 15 minutes
Makes 6 servings as a breakfast cereal

Bring water and 1 cup/8 fl oz/250 ml milk to the boil in a
2-qt/2-l saucepan; stir in oats, barley, brown sugar, cinnamon
and salt. Return to the boil; reduce heat. Cover and simmer for
5 minutes. Stir in dried fruit; cook for about 7 minutes longer,
or until barley is tender. Serve hot with milk, if desired, or
cover and refrigerate to serve later.

About Dried Fruit

Drying has been used as a means of preserving fruits for use out of season since ancient times. As well as conserving the nutritional value, drying introduces no extra sugar (as canning and bottling do) and also intensifies the flavor of many fruits. There is now a huge variety of dried fruits available, but it is also possible to dry your own. Apricots, figs, nectarines, peaches, pears and plums are all good candidates for home drying. Select fresh, firm fruit and wash carefully. Halve and pit, then remove any small imperfections with a sharp knife. Arrange fruit on racks, cut-side-up, and dry in a very cool oven, 120°F to 150°F/50°C to 65°C, for 6–24 hours, or until the skin is wrinkled and gentle squeezing produces no juice. Cool slowly and store in airtight containers in a cool dark place. For dried apple rings, peel and core apples and cut into rings about 1/4 in/6 mm thick. Immerse in salt water for a few minutes; remove and shake well. Thread onto dowel rods and suspend across baking dishes. Dry in a very cool oven, 120°F to 150°F/50°C to 65°C, for 6–12 hours, or until the slices resemble chamois and gentle squeezing produces no juice. Store in the same way as dried stone fruit.

If you live in a sunny area, you might prefer to sun-dry your harvest. If so, arrange the prepared fruit on racks, cover with cheesecloth (muslin) to protect from dust, and place in the sun, out of the reach of birds and mice, until well dried.

FRYING

Frying Vegetables and Grains

The methods of quick cooking covered in this chapter, all frying techniques, are easily executed on top of the stove. They use an open pan and varying amounts of fat to enhance the mild, naturally appealing flavor of vegetables and to marry grains and beans with the other ingredients.

Sautéing, a classic French technique, and stir-frying, an Asian method, are practically identical, except for the pans used. Both require minimal fat and the briefest of cooking times.

Vegetable sautés need brisk, frequent stirring in a wide pan with straight or slightly sloping sides that permit rapid motion. Stir-fries are tossed constantly in a wok, a deep pan with sloping sides.

Pan-fried recipes—such as potato pancakes and lentil patties—use slightly more fat and are turned once, to brown both sides.

Deep-fried tempura and other batter-coated vegetable items bob in a quantity of hot bubbling fat until golden outside and tender within.

BASIC TOOLS FOR FRYING VEGETABLES AND GRAINS

Pans for frying include a wok, a sauté pan or frying pan and
a deep, heavy saucepan or deep-fryer. Spoons and spatulas
keep foods in motion so they don't brown too much, while
a deep-fat thermometer monitors oil temperature. Use a
wire-mesh skimmer to remove cooked foods from fat.

heavy saucepan
and deep-fat
thermometer

wok and wok spatula

sauté pan and
wooden spatula

wire-mesh
skimmer

measuring
spoons

spatula

Use a straight-sided sauté pan like this one or a frying pan with sloping sides.

Before using the wok for the first time, season it according to the manufacturer's instructions.

Stir-frying is a popular and convenient way to combine vegetables and grains, as in classic fried-rice dishes.

1. Sautéing
Once the oil, margarine or butter is hot, add the vegetables to the pan. Stir vigorously and frequently with a wooden spoon or spatula until the pieces are crisp-tender.

2. Preparing the Wok
A seasoned wok requires less oil for cooking. Swirl a small amount of oil around the sides of the pan, starting at the top so the oil will flow to the bottom and coat the surface completely.

3. Stir-frying
With a long-handled stir-fry spatula or wooden spoon, lift and turn the vegetables with a folding motion. This rapid tossing exposes each piece of food to the hot, oil-coated cooking surface of the wok.

Instead of tossing and stirring the food, it is browned on one side and then turned.

Don't deep-fry too many pieces of food at a time or the oil temperature will drop and the pieces will stick together.

A quick stir-fry transforms carrots and celery, two year-round vegetables, into a colorful accompaniment for a week-day dinner. The recipe appears on page 111.

4. Pan-frying

Heat oil, margarine or butter in the pan, then arrange the food with some space between the pieces. The oil is at the proper temperature if it sizzles slightly when the food is added.

5. Deep-frying

Heat oil in a deep, heavy saucepan or deep-fryer to the temperature called for in the recipe (clip a deep-fat thermometer to side of pan with tip immersed in the fat). Cook a few batter-coated pieces at a time. When golden, remove with a wire skimmer.

Lentil Patties with Onions and Cheese Sauce

Lentils are a member of the legume family. They are a good source of protein and have a mild, nutty flavor and a rich, meaty texture.

INGREDIENTS

LENTIL PATTIES

4½ oz/140 g green or brown lentils

1⅓ cups/11 fl oz/345 ml water

1 egg

2 tablespoons milk

¾ oz/20 g toasted wheat germ

1 oz/30 g fine dry breadcrumbs

2 tablespoons tahini (sesame seed paste)

2 cloves garlic, minced

½ teaspoon salt

3 tablespoons olive oil

1 large red (Spanish) onion, sliced

CHEESE SAUCE

1 tablespoon margarine or butter

1 tablespoon plain flour

Pinch pepper

¾ cup/6 fl oz/190 ml milk

3 oz/90 g grated Swiss or mild melting cheese

These substantial lentil patties are enhanced with the exotic flavor of tahini, a Middle Eastern sesame seed paste.

Preparation time 20 minutes
Cooking time 40 to 50 minutes
Serves 4 as a main course

For lentil patties, rinse lentils. In a saucepan combine water and uncooked lentils. Bring to the boil; reduce heat. Cover and simmer for 30 minutes, or until tender. Drain lentils well.

Process lentils, egg and milk in a blender container or food processor bowl until nearly smooth. Transfer mixture to a medium mixing bowl. Add wheat germ, breadcrumbs, tahini, garlic and salt; stir until combined. Shape mixture into 4 patties, each about ½ in/1 cm thick.

Heat 1 tablespoon oil in a large frying pan. Cook onion for 3–5 minutes, or until tender. Remove onion, cover and keep warm. Add remaining oil and cook patties, turning once, for 5–7 minutes, or until golden brown all over.

Meanwhile, for sauce, melt margarine or butter in a small saucepan. Stir in flour and pepper. Add milk all at once. Cook and stir over medium heat until thickened and bubbly. Cook and stir for 1 minute more. Add cheese; stir over low heat until melted. Top each patty with onions and cheese sauce.

STEP 1

Making Patties
Put the puréed lentil mixture in a bowl. With a wooden spoon, stir in wheat germ, breadcrumbs, tahini, garlic and salt, then mix to combine thoroughly.

STEP 2

Shaping Patties
Pick up one quarter of the mixture with your hands. Pat and shape into a patty that is about ½ in/1 cm thick. Repeat with the remaining lentil mixture.

STEP 3

Thickening Sauce
When the butter or margarine has melted and the flour, milk and flavorings are stirred in, stir over medium heat until thickened and bubbly.

Potato Pancakes

These pancakes will vary in tone from cream to gold to orange depending on the flesh color of the potatoes or sweet potatoes used. Choose any good frying potato from the many varieties now available. Sweet potatoes add not only bright color but also lots of vitamin A.

INGREDIENTS

12 oz/375 g potatoes or sweet potatoes, peeled and coarsely grated

1 medium onion, finely chopped

3 eggs, lightly beaten

2 tablespoons all-purpose (plain) flour

1 teaspoon salt

¼ teaspoon pepper

3 tablespoons cooking oil

Sour cream

Apple sauce or lightly sweetened cooked apple purée

For a delicate sweetness and irresistible crunch, make these potato pancakes using sweet potatoes.

Preparation time 15 minutes
Cooking time 15 minutes
Serves 4 as an accompaniment

Combine grated potato, onion and eggs in a large mixing bowl. Add flour, salt and pepper; stir until combined.

Heat 2 tablespoons of the oil in a large frying pan. Spoon pancake batter into frying pan, using about ¼ cup/2 fl oz/60 ml batter for each pancake. Cook, turning once, for about 5 minutes, or until golden brown. Add additional oil as necessary during cooking. Drain on paper towels.

Keep pancakes warm in a preheated 300°F/150°C/Gas Mark 2 oven while cooking remaining pancakes. Serve hot with sour cream and apple sauce or puréed apple.

Frying

STEP 1

Grating Potatoes

Grip a peeled potato firmly in one hand and secure a box grater on a sheet of waxed paper with the other. Move the potato up and down over the grater's large holes to grate the flesh coarsely.

STEP 2

Cooking Pancakes

Heat oil in a frying pan. For each pancake, add about ¼ cup/ 2 fl oz/60 ml potato batter to the hot oil. Flatten slightly with the back of a small spatula or egg-lifter. When brown on one side, lift and turn over to brown the other side.

Corn Fritters

Because these corn fritters are rounded in shape, they are often called
"corn oysters" in their native New England, where they are
a popular vegetable accompaniment. The fresher the corn,
the better the flavor of these delicious little nuggets.

INGREDIENTS

3 large cobs of corn

2 egg yolks

4 teaspoons all-purpose
(plain) flour

4 teaspoons cornstarch
(cornflour)

1 teaspoon sugar

½ teaspoon salt

¼ teaspoon pepper

2 egg whites

3 to 4 tablespoons cooking oil

METHOD FOR MAKING CORN FRITTERS

*Make these light,
golden nuggets in
summer when corn is
at its seasonal best.*

Preparation time 30 minutes
Cooking time 20 to 25 minutes
Makes 4 to 5 servings as an accompaniment (20 to 24 fritters)

Remove husks and silk from fresh cobs of corn. Rinse and pat dry.
With a sharp knife, cut kernels from cobs to obtain 9 oz/280 g corn.

Beat egg yolks in a small mixing bowl with an electric mixer on high
speed for about 5 minutes, or until thick and lemon colored. Stir in
corn, flour, cornflour, sugar, salt and pepper.

Wash and dry beaters thoroughly. Beat egg whites in a medium
mixing bowl on high speed until stiff peaks form (tips stand straight
up). Gently fold egg whites into the corn mixture.

Heat 2 tablespoons oil in a large frying pan; add batter by generous
tablespoons. Fry fritters, a few at a time, over medium heat for
5–6 minutes, or until they are golden brown and crisp; turn once
and adding remaining oil as necessary. As fritters are cooked, transfer
them to a heated platter; keep warm in a preheated oven, 300°F/
150°C/Gas Mark 2, until all are cooked. Serve warm.

STEP 1

Removing Kernels

Strip husks from corn cobs and remove silk. Trim off tip to flatten and stand cob on flat end. With a long, sharp knife, cut off kernels without cutting into the cob.

STEP 2

Beating Egg Yolks

Beat egg yolks in a mixing bowl on high speed until they thicken and change in appearance from orange-yellow to a pale lemon color. They should fall from the beater in a ribbon.

About Cooking Corn Cobs

Regardless of which of the many varieties of corn you are cooking, freshness is the key to producing a tender and succulent vegetable for the table. If you have access to freshly picked cobs, perhaps from your garden, bring a large pot of unsalted water to the boil, add the cobs, with husks intact or not, as you prefer. (However, if you must store the cobs, leave them in their husks until the last moment before cooking so they don't dry out.) Simmer for only about 5 minutes. If the corn is not quite so fresh, simmer for up to 15 minutes, or until the kernels feel tender when pierced with a sharp knife or skewer.

Corn cobs are also excellent grilled (barbecued) (*see pages 170–171*). The smoky charred taste imparted by the grill adds another dimension to the flavor.

Quick Tomato Sauce

This fresh-tasting tomato sauce cooks in less than one hour. It will have its freshest flavor when served within a few hours of preparation, but it can be covered and refrigerated for one or two days or frozen for up to two weeks and still be delicious. If you like, add garlic and herbs and/or a few tablespoons of red or white wine to the sauce near the end of the cooking time.

INGREDIENTS

2 tablespoons extra virgin olive oil or sunflower or canola oil

1 ¼ oz/40 g finely chopped yellow onion

Minced garlic (optional)

Minced fresh or dried herbs (optional)

36 oz/1.1 kg peeled, seeded, chopped and well-drained plum (Roma) tomatoes, fresh or canned

Salt and freshly ground white pepper

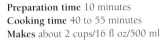

Preparation time 10 minutes
Cooking time 40 to 55 minutes
Makes about 2 cups/16 fl oz/500 ml

Warm oil in a saucepan over low heat. Add onion and cook for 4 to 5 minutes, or until translucent; do not allow to brown. Add garlic and herbs to taste (or as directed for individual recipes) and cook for about 1 minute, or until fragrant.

Add tomatoes and bring to the boil over high heat. Reduce heat and simmer, uncovered, stirring occasionally, for 30–35 minutes for canned tomatoes, 40–45 minutes for fresh tomatoes, or until the juices have evaporated and the sauce has thickened.

Season to taste with salt and pepper; use immediately, or let cool, cover and refrigerate or freeze.

Stuffed Zucchini Flowers with Tomato–Mint Sauce

Gentle cooking brings out the delightful peppery flavor of fresh zucchini flowers.
In this simple preparation, the tender blossoms are filled with sheep milk cheese, then
accented with a refreshing tomato–mint sauce. If you prefer, substitute mozzarella
or Fontina for the caciotta or provolone cheese.

INGREDIENTS

16 zucchini (courgette) flowers, slightly closed

4 oz/125 g caciotta or provolone cheese, rind removed

1½ oz/45 g all-purpose (plain) flour

¼ cup/2 fl oz/45 ml sunflower or safflower oil

TOMATO–MINT SAUCE

1 cup/8 fl oz/250 ml Quick Tomato Sauce (see recipe on page 106)

2 large fresh mint leaves, thinly sliced, or ⅛ teaspoon dried mint

Preparation time
about 15 minutes
Cooking time
10 minutes
Makes 4 servings

Trim off long stems and carefully spread flower petals slightly apart. Cut cheese into 16 rectangles ½ in/1 cm wide by ½ in/1 cm thick by 1 in/2.5 cm long, or long enough to fit snugly inside the flowers. Place 1 piece of cheese inside each flower and close the petals over.

Spread flour on a plate. Gently roll each flower in the flour, carefully turning to coat lightly but evenly. Transfer to a clean plate.

Heat oil in a large frying pan over medium heat. Add stuffed flowers in a single layer and cook for 2–3 minutes. Using 2 forks, turn flowers over and cook the other side for 1–2 minutes longer, or until flowers are golden brown on the edges and the cheese has begun to melt. The flowers should remain soft.

Meanwhile, make the sauce (*see page 106*) or, if already prepared, reheat. Add mint and simmer for 1 minute.

Using 2 forks, remove flowers from the pan, draining off any excess oil. Arrange 4 flowers on each of 4 warmed plates with the stem ends toward the center. Spoon the sauce over the stem ends only and serve immediately.

Sesame Celery and Carrot Sauté

Toasting enhances the color and flavor of sesame seeds: spread them in a thin layer in an ungreased shallow baking dish and bake in a preheated oven, 350°F/180°C/Gas Mark 4, stirring once or twice, for 10 minutes, or until light golden brown.

INGREDIENTS

1 tablespoon margarine or butter

6 oz/185 g thinly bias-sliced peeled carrots (3 medium)

6 oz/185 g thinly sliced celery (4 stalks)

1 to 2 teaspoons honey

2 teaspoons sesame seeds

¼ teaspoon salt

Preparation time 10 minutes
Cooking time 6 to 7 minutes
Makes 4 servings as an accompaniment

Melt margarine or butter in a large frying pan. Cook carrots over medium-high heat for 1 minute, stirring frequently. Add celery and cook, stirring frequently, for 4–5 minutes, or until vegetables are crisp-tender. Stir in honey to taste, sesame seeds and salt.

When cut into colorful ovals and pretty half-moons, carrots and celery make an elegant pair in this quick main-course accompaniment.

Dilled Cucumbers and Tomatoes

Remember this light, crunchy dish when you need a quick way to use
up a bumper crop of cucumbers and tomatoes. You can stir-fry the whole dish
in less than five minutes.

INGREDIENTS

2 medium cucumbers, peeled

1 tablespoon peanut or
cooking oil

1 oz/30 g sliced green
(spring) onion

1 clove garlic, minced

6 oz/185 g cherry tomatoes,
stemmed and halved

2 teaspoons finely chopped
fresh dill or ½ teaspoon
dried dillweed

⅛ teaspoon salt

⅛ teaspoon pepper

Cucumbers and tomatoes are naturals for salads, but when briefly stir-fried with garlic and dill, they make a satisfying hot side dish.

Preparation time about 15 minutes
Cooking time 5 minutes
Makes 4 to 6 servings as an accompaniment

Halve cucumbers along their length. With the tip of a spoon, remove seeds. Slice cucumbers across into ¼-in/6-mm-thick slices. (You should have about 12 to 13 oz/375 to 410 g.)

Heat oil in a wok or frying pan. Add green onion and garlic and stir-fry for 30 seconds. Add cucumber and stir-fry for about 3 minutes, or until crisp-tender. Stir in tomatoes, dill, salt and pepper. Cover and cook for 1 minute more, or until heated through. Serve at once.

Frying

STEP 1

Seeding Cucumbers

Peel the cucumbers and cut in half along their length.
With the tip of a spoon, scrape down the center from top
to bottom to scoop out the seeds. Repeat with other halves.

STEP 2

Slicing Cucumbers

Place one peeled, seeded cucumber half on a cutting
board, cut-side-down. With a sharp knife, slice across into
half-moons, cutting on the diagonal, if desired, to create a
bias cut.

Tempura Vegetables with Dipping Sauce

To minimize spattering when making tempura, be sure vegetables
are dry before coating them in batter. Fry only a few pieces at a
time to prevent them from sticking together.

INGREDIENTS

SAUCE

3 tablespoons soy sauce

2 tablespoons orange juice

2 tablespoons dry sherry

1 tablespoon finely chopped
green (spring) onion

1 teaspoon sugar

1 teaspoon sesame seeds

Few splashes bottled hot chili
sauce

TEMPURA

7 oz/220 g all-purpose (plain)
flour

¼ teaspoon bicarbonate of soda

⅛ teaspoon salt

1 egg yolk, beaten

13 fl oz/410 ml ice water

Peanut oil or cooking oil, for
deep frying

1 lb/500 g cut-up mixed fresh
vegetables, such as 1-in/2.5-cm
pieces of asparagus, green beans
or Chinese long beans; sliced and
peeled carrots, sweet or white
potatoes or parsnips; broccoli
florets; halved mushrooms; sliced
zucchini (courgettes) or slender
eggplant (aubergine); and/or bell
pepper (capsicum) strips

Tempura batter gives a light, crunchy coating to fresh vegetables. Serve with a piquant dipping sauce.

Preparation time 15 minutes
Cooking time 8 to 12 minutes
Makes 12 servings as a
first course

Combine the soy sauce, orange juice, sherry, green onion, sugar, sesame seeds and hot chili sauce in a small mixing bowl. Set the dipping sauce aside.

For tempura, combine flour with bicarbonate of soda and salt in a medium mixing bowl. Make a well in the center. Combine egg yolk and ice water; add, all at once, to flour mixture. Stir just until combined (a few lumps should remain).

Heat 2 to 3 in/5 to 7.5 cm of oil to 365°F/185°C in a deep, heavy saucepan or deep fryer. Dip completely dry vegetables into batter, a few pieces at a time, swirling to coat. Fry a few pieces at a time in hot oil for 2–3 minutes, or until golden, turning once. Remove vegetables from oil with a wire skimmer or slotted spoon.

Drain on a wok rack or on paper towels. Keep warm in a preheated oven, 300°F/150°C/Gas Mark 2, while frying remaining pieces. Serve warm with the dipping sauce.

Stir-Fried Rice with Vegetables

Choose from long-grain white, brown or wild rice, and allow more cooking time for brown or wild rice. You may even want to cook the rice a day ahead to save time when you're ready to stir-fry.

INGREDIENTS

2 cups/16 fl oz/500 ml water

7 oz/220 g long-grain white or brown rice, or 6 oz/185 g wild rice, rinsed and drained

3 tablespoons peanut oil

2 eggs, beaten

10 oz/315 g cut-up mixed fresh vegetables, such as sliced mushrooms; thinly sliced peeled water chestnuts; julienne strips of bell pepper (capsicum), jícama

(yam bean), or zucchini (courgettes); snow peas (mangetout), cut in half; bean sprouts; broccoli florets; cubed radish or daikon; and/or sliced carrots

2 green (spring) onions, sliced

1 clove garlic, minced

⅛ teaspoon crushed dried chili

2 tablespoons soy sauce

2 tablespoons dry sherry

Preparation time 15 minutes
Cooking time 25 to 50 minutes
Makes 6 servings as an accompaniment

Bring water to the boil in a medium saucepan. Add uncooked rice, return to the boil, reduce heat. Cover and simmer until rice is tender and water is absorbed, allowing 15 minutes for long-grain white rice, 35 minutes for brown rice and 40 minutes for wild rice. Remove from heat. Let stand, covered, for 5 minutes. Set aside.

Heat 1 tablespoon of the oil in a wok or frying pan. Add beaten egg and cook, without stirring, for about 2 minutes, or until set. Invert pan to remove egg; cut into strips. Set aside.

Add 1 tablespoon oil to the same pan and stir-fry desired vegetables until crisp-tender. Allow 1–2 minutes for mushrooms, water chestnuts, pepper, jícama, zucchini, snow peas and bean sprouts; 3–4 minutes for broccoli, radish or daikon; and 4–5 minutes for carrots. Remove from wok.

Add remaining 1 tablespoon oil; stir-fry green onion, garlic and crushed dried chili for 30 seconds. Add rice and cook for 2 minutes more. Return egg strips and cooked vegetables to wok; add soy sauce and sherry. Cover and cook for 2 minutes more, or until heated through. Serve immediately.

If the rice and other ingredients are ready next to the cooktop, this colorful stir-fry can be finished in minutes.

Sautéed Mushrooms with Onion, Garlic and Parsley

Use a mixture of fresh mushrooms, including white mushrooms, portobellos, cremini and any wild varieties that are available. Serve as a side dish or with bruschetta.

INGREDIENTS

¾ oz/20 g dried porcini

1 cup/8 fl oz/250 ml cool water

1 tablespoon extra-virgin olive oil

2 tablespoons minced yellow onion

1 tablespoon minced garlic

1 lb/500 g assorted fresh mushrooms, stems removed, brushed clean and sliced

3 tablespoons chopped fresh parsley

¼ cup/2 fl oz/60 ml dry Italian white wine

Salt and freshly ground pepper

METHOD FOR MAKING SAUTEED MUSHROOMS
WITH ONION, GARLIC AND PARSLEY

Preparation time 15 minutes
Standing time 20 minutes
Cooking time 20 minutes
Makes 4 servings

Combine porcini and water in a bowl and stand for about 20 minutes, or until softened. Remove porcini, reserving liquid. Clean porcini, if necessary, and chop coarsely. Strain the porcini liquid through a fine-mesh sieve lined with cheesecloth (muslin) into a clean container, then discard all but ¼ cup/2 fl oz/60 ml of the liquid.

Heat olive oil in a frying pan over medium heat. Add onion and garlic and cook for about 30 seconds, or until fragrant; do not allow to brown. Add porcini and fresh mushrooms and continue to cook over medium heat, stirring constantly to prevent burning, for about 3 minutes, or until slightly limp.

Add the ¼ cup/2 fl oz/60 ml of reserved porcini liquid and simmer for 3 minutes. Add the parsley and white wine and simmer over medium heat for 8–10 minutes, or until there is only about ¼ cup/2 fl oz/ 60 ml liquid remaining.

Season to taste with salt and pepper. Transfer to a warmed serving dish and serve immediately.

Broccoli–Noodle Stir-Fry

Thin noodles look best in this sesame-flavored stir-fry. Look for fine noodles, nested vermicelli or capellini in the Asian foods or pasta section of your supermarket.

INGREDIENTS

3 oz/90 g dried fine noodles

SAUCE

⅔ cup/5 fl oz/160 ml vegetable stock

2 teaspoons cornflour

1½ teaspoons soy sauce

1 teaspoon rice vinegar or white vinegar

⅛ to ¼ teaspoon crushed dried chilies

1 tablespoon cooking oil

2 teaspoons toasted sesame oil

10 oz/315 g broccoli florets

Preparation time 10 minutes
Cooking time 10 to 12 minutes
Makes 6 servings as an
accompaniment

Bring 8 cups/64 fl oz/2 l of water to the boil in a large saucepan. Add noodles and boil, uncovered, stirring occasionally, for 5–7 minutes, or until just tender. (Or, cook according to package directions.) Drain.

Meanwhile, for sauce, combine stock, cornflour, soy sauce, vinegar and crushed dried chilies in a small bowl. Set aside.

Heat cooking oil and sesame oil in a wok or large frying pan over medium-high heat. Add broccoli; stir-fry for 3–4 minutes, or until crisp-tender. Stir sauce; add sauce and cooked noodles to wok or frying pan. Cook, stirring, until thickened and bubbly. Cook, stirring, for 1 minute more. Serve immediately.

Rich, aromatic sesame oil perfumes a lightly tossed mixture of broccoli florets and slender noodles.

Zucchini Fritters

Although these fritters are at their best piping hot, they are often also served in Turkish cafés at room temperature with a yogurt–cucumber sauce. They are traditionally part of the meze course.

INGREDIENTS

1 lb/500 g small zucchini (courgettes), coarsely grated

Salt

8 oz/250 g feta cheese, or equal parts feta and kasseri or ricotta

6 green (spring) onions, chopped

3 tablespoons chopped fresh dill

2 tablespoons chopped fresh mint

2 tablespoons chopped fresh flat-leaf (Italian) parsley

3 eggs, lightly beaten

1 1/4 cups/5 oz/155 g all-purpose (plain) flour

Freshly ground pepper

Peanut oil, for frying

These delicious zucchini fritters are usually served with an array of similar appealing morsels as part of a Middle-Eastern meze course to whet the appetite.

Preparation time 5 to 10 minutes
Standing time 30 minutes
Cooking time 5 to 10 minutes
Makes 8 servings as an appetizer
or 4 as a side dish

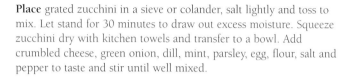

Place grated zucchini in a sieve or colander, salt lightly and toss to mix. Let stand for 30 minutes to draw out excess moisture. Squeeze zucchini dry with kitchen towels and transfer to a bowl. Add crumbled cheese, green onion, dill, mint, parsley, egg, flour, salt and pepper to taste and stir until well mixed.

Heat oil to a depth of ¼ in/6 mm in a deep frying pan over medium-high heat. Drop spoonfuls of batter into the hot oil, being careful not to crowd the pan. Cook, turning once, for 2–3 minutes on each side, or until nicely browned on both sides.

Using a slotted spoon or spatula, transfer fritters to paper towels to drain. Keep warm until all fritters are cooked.

Arrange fritters on a warmed platter and serve hot. Can also be served at room temperature with a dipping sauce, such as Peanut Satay Sauce (*see page 187*).

Southwestern Bean and Corn Tacos

Tortillas are easier to fold if you warm them first. To warm, wrap them
in foil and heat in a 350°F/180°C/Gas Mark 4 oven for 10 minutes. Or wrap them in
paper towels and microwave for a few seconds on high power.

INGREDIENTS

FILLING

7 oz/220 g dried black, red kidney or garbanzo beans (chick-peas) or 12 oz/375 g tinned beans, drained and rinsed

8 cups/64 fl oz/2 l water

1 tablespoon cooking oil

6 oz/185 g finely chopped zucchini (courgettes) or yellow summer (baby) squash

6 oz/185 g fresh or frozen corn kernels

2 cloves garlic, minced

1 fresh mild green chili or 1 tinned green chili, drained, seeded and finely chopped

1 small hot chili, seeded and chopped (optional)

1 oz/30 g shredded jícama (yam bean) (optional)

FRESH SALSA

6 oz/185 g finely chopped peeled tomatoes (2 medium)

¾ oz/25 g sliced green (spring) onion

2 tablespoons lemon juice

2 tablespoons chopped fresh cilantro (coriander/Chinese parsley)

1 clove garlic, minced

Several splashes hot chili sauce

TACOS

4 oz/125 g shredded lettuce

8 flour tortillas, each 10 in/25 cm in diameter, or packaged taco shells, warmed (see headnote)

4 oz/125 g grated mild melting cheese or Cheddar cheese

Sour cream

133

Preparation time 20 minutes
Standing time 1 hour to overnight
Cooking time 1 to 2 hours
Makes 4 servings as a main course
(2 tacos each)

For filling (if using dried beans),
rinse beans. In a 16-cup/4-qt/4-l
saucepan combine dried beans
and 4 cups/32 fl oz/1 l of water.
Bring to the boil; reduce heat
and simmer for 2 minutes.
Remove from heat. Cover and let
stand for 1 hour. (Or omit
simmering: soak by placing
beans in 4 cups/32 fl oz/1 l
water in a 16-cup/4-qt/4-l
saucepan. Cover and leave in a
cool place for 6–8 hours or
overnight.) Drain beans and
rinse. (If using red kidney beans,
boil for 10 minutes in water to
cover; drain again.) In the same
pan combine beans and
remaining 4 cups/32 fl oz/1 l
water. Bring to the boil; reduce
heat. Cover and simmer, stirring
occasionally, for 1–2 hours, or
until beans are tender. Drain.

Heat oil in a large frying pan,
add zucchini or squash, corn,
garlic and chilies. Cook, stirring,
for 5 minutes. Stir in cooked or
tinned beans and jícama, if
desired; cook and stir until
heated through.

Combine tomato with green
onion, lemon juice, cilantro,
garlic and hot chili sauce to taste
in a mixing bowl. Set salsa aside.

For tacos, sprinkle shredded
lettuce in the center of a flour
tortilla. Top with some of the
bean filling, grated cheese, sour
cream and fresh salsa. Fold the
bottom edge of each tortilla up
and over filling. Fold in opposite
sides of each tortilla to overlap
slightly, leaving one end open.
Serve immediately. If using
packaged taco shells, heat them
according to the directions on
the packet and fill as before.

Soft tortillas enclose a spicy filling of golden corn and other colorful vegetables.

Sautéed Spinach with Almonds and Raisins

Many cultures make use of dark, leafy spinach as a hearty side dish. Combined with almonds and raisins, and given a spark of flavor from fresh ginger, this version is reminiscent of Middle Eastern cuisines.

INGREDIENTS

1 lb/500 g spinach

1 tablespoon olive oil

1 tablespoon margarine or butter

1½ oz/45 g flaked almonds or pine nuts

2 oz/60 g sultanas or raisins

1 teaspoon grated ginger root

¼ teaspoon salt

Pinch of pepper

Deep-green spinach retains its color and nutrients when briefly sautéed in a little oil. Almonds, raisins and pungent ginger add highlights of texture and taste.

Preparation time 20 minutes
Cooking time 8 to 10 minutes
Makes 4 to 6 servings as an accompaniment

Wash and drain spinach; remove stems. Heat olive oil and melt margarine or butter in a 12-in/30-cm frying pan or wok. Add almonds or pine nuts, sultanas or raisins, ginger and salt; cook, stirring, for 3 minutes, or until nuts are golden brown. Remove from pan with a slotted spoon.

Cook spinach in the same pan, stirring frequently, for 3–5 minutes, or until wilted. Stir in almond mixture and pepper. Serve immediately.

About Almonds

The almond tree has been valued for its nutritious nut for thousands of years. Not surprisingly, the delicately flavored almond turns up in all courses, from roasted and salted as a snack to the most elegant dessert, in most of the world's cuisines.

Storing Almonds are sold whole, roasted, salted, blanched, halved, slivered, flaked, chopped, ground or in the form of a paste. They keep best in their shells, but as they are readily available year-round, you may prefer to buy them as you need them and in the form you need them for particular purposes. For example, buy only small quantities of ground almonds, or almond meal, for cakes and biscuits and use quickly. You can buy larger quantities of whole, unblanched almonds, which are protected by their skins. Always store in an airtight container in the refrigerator or some other cool place.

To Blanch Almonds Place nuts in a bowl, pour on enough boiling water to cover generously and stand for 5 minutes. Drain and rinse with cold water. As you press each kernel between your thumb and forefinger, the brown skin will slip off easily. Dry kernels on a clean tea towel before use.

Eggs Scrambled with Tortillas, Beans and Salsa

Popular throughout the American Southwest, this dish, known as *migas*, features the robust flavors common to Mexican cooking. Accompany with a glass of chilled orange juice infused with prickly pear juice for a genuine experience of the region's food.

INGREDIENTS

1 fresh poblano chili

3 corn tortillas, each 6 in/15 cm in diameter

3 fl oz/100 ml corn oil

8 flour tortillas, each 8 in/20 cm in diameter

1 cup/8 oz/250 g refried beans (see recipe page 143)

2 oz/60 g white onion, chopped

1 fresh jalapeño chili, seeded and finely diced

2 teaspoons chopped fresh cilantro (coriander/Chinese parsley) leaves, plus sprigs for garnish

8 eggs, beaten

¾ teaspoon salt

4 oz/125 g Monterey Jack cheese, shredded

1 cup/8 fl oz/250 ml bottled salsa

The ingredients needed for this dish are all easy to find at Latino food markets.

METHOD FOR MAKING EGGS SCRAMBLED WITH TORTILLAS, BEANS AND SALSA

Preparation time about 10 minutes
Cooking time about 10 minutes
Makes 4 servings

Preheat a broiler (grill) and broil the poblano chili, turning, until charred on all sides. Cool for 5 minutes, then peel off skin under cold running water. Cut chili into small strips.

Stack corn tortillas and cut in halves. Cut the halves into narrow triangular strips. Heat oil in a non-stick frying pan over medium heat. Add tortilla pieces and sauté for about 30 seconds, or until slightly crisp. Using tongs or a slotted spoon, transfer to paper towels to drain. Reserve the oil and pan for later use.

Toast flour tortillas on both sides in a dry frying pan over medium heat. Keep warm. Reheat beans in a small saucepan. Keep warm.

Cook onion in reserved pan and oil for about 3 minutes, or until just tender. Add tortilla triangles, both the chilies and chopped cilantro. Cook briefly, then add beaten egg and salt. Stir with a wooden spoon for 10 seconds. Add half the cheese and cook, stirring, for 15–20 seconds longer, or until the eggs are tender and just set.

Serve immediately with beans, flour tortillas and salsa. Sprinkle with remaining cheese and garnish with cilantro sprigs.

Refried Beans

No Mexican meal is complete without this creamy staple. Although pinto beans
fried in lard are the more traditional choice, black beans fried in vegetable oil are now
more acceptable to the health-conscious. These beans go best with rice.

INGREDIENTS

14 oz/440 g dried black or
pinto beans

8 cups/64 fl oz/2 l water

5 oz/155 g lard or ⅔ cup/5 fl oz/
160 ml vegetable oil

1 large yellow onion, diced

1 to 2 teaspoons salt

½ teaspoon freshly ground pepper

Fresh cilantro (coriander/Chinese
parsley) leaves (optional), for
garnish

Mexican refried beans and steamed rice make an unbeatable partnership.

Preparation time 10 minutes
Cooking time about 2 hours
Makes 4 to 6 servings as an
accompaniment

Sort through beans and discard any stones, or broken or misshapen beans. Rinse well. Place beans in a saucepan, add the water and bring to the boil. Reduce heat, cover and simmer for about 1½ hours, or until the smallest beans are cooked through and creamy inside.

Remove beans from the heat. Using a potato masher, mash beans, with the remaining cooking liquid, until evenly mashed.

Heat lard or oil in a sauté pan over medium heat. Add all but about 2 tablespoons of the diced onion and cook briskly for about 10 minutes, or until the onion is translucent and beginning to brown. Add mashed beans and cook, stirring, until excess liquid evaporates and beans start to pull away from sides of pan. Cook, without stirring, until a thin crust begins to stick to the pan. Scrape up the crust and reincorporate into the beans. Repeat this step several times, until the beans are thick and creamy. Season to taste.

Note: Store any leftover beans, covered, in the refrigerator for up to 4 days. When reheating, add a little water to the pan and heat beans, stirring constantly, over medium heat.

Spoon beans onto a warmed platter or individual plates and top with reserved onion. Garnish with cilantro, if desired, and serve hot.

GRILLING AND BROILING

Steps for Grilling and Broiling Vegetables and Grains

Broiling (known in Europe as grilling) and its twin method, grilling (also known as barbecuing), blast vegetables with dry radiant heat at a very high temperature. In minutes, tough fibers soften and tenderize with magnificent results: bell peppers (capsicums) develop a smoky intensity, onions mellow, eggplant (aubergine) turns creamy.

Grilling vegetables is no different from grilling other foods. If the grill is too crowded, or if broiling indoors is more convenient, most of the recipes in this chapter can be broiled. Vegetables cook quickly, which is one reason for their appeal. But, bombarded with heat from glowing coals beneath or from the broiler's element above, they also can shrivel and dry out in an instant. Success is a harmony of time, temperature and distance from heat that requires your full attention to orchestrate.

Preparation is also critical. Cook pieces that are of similar size together. Make slices evenly thick, and keep chunks for skewers uniform. For added flavor and to retain moisture, immerse in an aromatic seasoned marinade or brush surfaces with a flavored oil (see page 153). You will find many wonderful grilled or broiled dishes in the pages ahead. Marinating also keeps food from sticking, as does preheating the grill rack and oiling it lightly. An alternative is to enclose whole or cut-up vegetables in a foil package and steam them on the grill in their natural juices or in added liquid.

As a group, grains and beans are better cooked in other ways—with a few delicious exceptions. When both grain and vegetable are infused with smoky grilled flavor, the result is like Italian cuisine at its simple best.

BASIC TOOLS FOR GRILLING AND BROILING

Use a broiler pan with a slotted rack for broiling, a brush, bowls, dishes and a screw-top jar for marinades and bastes, and long-handled tongs to keep your hands at a safe distance from the heat. Skewers keep foods together on the grill and a ruler is helpful when positioning the broiler pan.

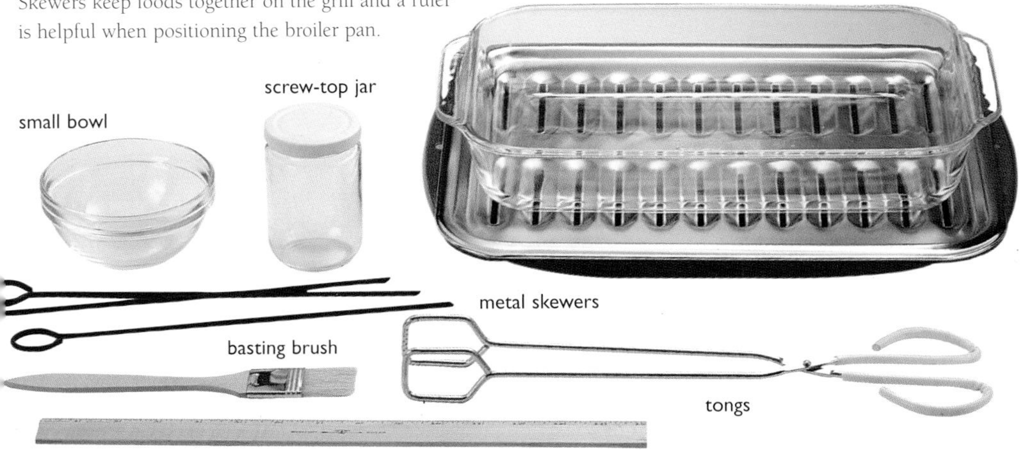

marinating dish and
broiler pan with rack

screw-top jar

small bowl

metal skewers

basting brush

tongs

ruler

Ignite as directed, depending on the type of charcoal used.

STEP 1

Preparing Coals

About 30 minutes before cooking, build a pyramid of barbecue charcoal in the center of the lower grate. To determine how much to use, make a single layer that extends past the cooking area, then pile up the pieces.

The coals are medium-hot when you can hold your hand 4 to 6 in/10 to 15 cm from the fire for 4 seconds.

STEP 2

Spreading Coals

Once the coals are medium-hot and covered with gray ash, use long-handled tongs to spread them in a single layer across the grate. To disperse the heat evenly, arrange the coals with about ½ in/2 cm of space between the pieces.

The heating element usually preheats within 10 minutes.

STEP 3

Broiling

Set the oven rack or adjustable broiler rack so the top of the food is 4 to 6 in/10 to 15 cm from the heating element, or as specified in the recipe. Remove rack with food and preheat the broiler.

Brushing with a sauce, marinade or herbed oil keeps the vegetables moist and adds flavor.

STEP 4

Brushing with Sauce

Arrange the vegetables on the unheated rack of a broiler pan and brush with sauce, marinade or flavored oil, making sure that they are completely coated so they won't dry out. Reserve some of the sauce and brush the vegetables several more times during cooking.

Leave some room between the top of the food and the foil to accommodate the steam that will form.

STEP 5

Making a Foil Packet

After spooning the food into the center of a double thickness of aluminum foil, bring the two opposite sides together. Fold the sides down twice to make a tight seal, leaving some room for steam to collect, then seal the ends to form an airtight package.

Turn the food occasionally to keep it constantly coated with marinade.

STEP 6

Marinating

Arrange the food in a non-aluminum baking dish. Mix the marinade in a jar with a screw-top lid and shake to combine. Pour the marinade over to coat all the ingredients completely. Set aside to marinate for the amount of time specified in the recipe.

About Flavored Oils

For interesting flavor notes, use herbed or flavored oils to brush on vegetables before grilling or barbecuing. They are very simple to prepare, so experiment with different herbs, garlic and chilies and always keep a selection on hand. Make them in smaller quantities unless you can use them within about a month of making.

Herbed Olive Oil Place 6 whole black peppercorns, 3 cloves garlic, crushed, 6 sprigs rosemary, 3 bay leaves, 2 sprigs fresh thyme and 2 sprigs fresh oregano in a sterilized 4-cup/32-fl-oz/1-l bottle. Pour in about 4 cups/32 fl oz/1 l of good-quality extra-virgin olive oil, ensuring that all the herbs are completely covered. Seal, label and store in the refrigerator for about 10 days before using. Keeps for about 1 month.

Grilled Romaine Salad with Chili Vinaigrette

Get fired up for a really hot salad: romaine (cos) lettuce quarters threaded onto skewers and grilled over medium-hot coals. The chili vinaigrette adds a different kind of heat. If using bamboo skewers, be sure to soak them for 30 minutes in advance.

INGREDIENTS

CHILI VINAIGRETTE

¼ cup/2 fl oz/60 ml red wine vinegar

¼ cup/2 fl oz/60 ml olive oil

1 clove garlic, minced

½ teaspoon salt

¼ to ½ teaspoon chili powder

¼ teaspoon pepper

SALAD

1 head romaine (cos) lettuce (about 1 lb/500 g)

2 oz/60 g Gorgonzola, blue or feta cheese, crumbled

1 oz/30 g broken pecans or walnuts, toasted

Wedges of ruffled romaine (cos) lettuce are enhanced by a few smoky minutes on the grill, then sliced for salad and dressed with a fiery vinaigrette.

METHOD FOR MAKING GRILLED ROMAINE SALAD WITH CHILI VINAIGRETTE

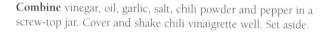

Preparation time 15 minutes
(plus 30 minutes for coals to heat)
Cooking time 3 to 5 minutes
Makes 6 servings as an
accompaniment

Combine vinegar, oil, garlic, salt, chili powder and pepper in a
screw-top jar. Cover and shake chili vinaigrette well. Set aside.

For salad, cut the lettuce lengthwise into quarters. To keep leaves
together, spear the wedges across with 3 metal or pre-soaked
bamboo skewers. Cook on an uncovered grill directly over medium-
hot coals, turning once, for 3–5 minutes, or until lettuce is wilted
and lightly charred.

Remove from grill. Remove skewers; trim off bottom core of each
lettuce wedge. Cut each wedge across into slices. Place lettuce in a
large salad bowl; add cheese and nuts. Shake dressing; pour over
salad. Toss salad and serve immediately.

Grilling and Broiling

STEP I

Cutting Lettuce

Place the washed and dried head of lettuce on a cutting surface. With a long, sharp knife, slice the head in half lengthwise. Then place each half cut-side-down and cut it in half again from top to bottom.

STEP 2

Skewering

Secure the leaves of each quarter section by inserting skewers across the wedge perpendicular to the core. If you are using bamboo skewers, soak them in water for 30 minutes before preparing lettuce for grilling.

Three-Pepper Open Sandwiches with Mozzarella

Look in the market during late summer to find bargain prices on a rainbow of bell peppers (capsicums). In the off season, make these sandwiches with green bell peppers.

INGREDIENTS

2 small red or orange bell peppers (capsicums)

2 small yellow or purple bell peppers (capsicums)

2 small green bell peppers (capsicums)

4 large slices sourdough bread

4 thin slices red (Spanish) or sweet white onion

1 tablespoon bottled Italian salad dressing or 1 tablespoon olive oil mixed with 1/4 teaspoon dried oregano

6 oz/185 g mozzarella, Swiss or mild melting cheese

2 tablespoons sliced, pitted black olives

Roasted peppers (capsicums) in three bright shades add color and substance to a layered open sandwich topped with melted mozzarella cheese.

METHOD FOR MAKING THREE-PEPPER OPEN SANDWICHES WITH MOZZARELLA

Preparation time 25 minutes
(plus 30 minutes for coals to heat)
Cooking time 12 to 16 minutes
Makes 4 servings as a main course

Halve bell peppers from stem to base; remove cores and seeds. Place halves, skin-side-down, on an uncovered grill rack directly over medium-hot coals. Cook for 8–10 minutes, or until skins are evenly charred. (Or, preheat broiler. Place halves, skin-side-up, on an unheated rack of the broiler pan. Cook peppers 4 in/10 cm from the heat for 8–10 minutes.)

Remove peppers from heat. Place halves in a brown paper bag; close bag. Let stand for 10–15 minutes to steam off skins. When cool, remove and discard skins. Cut peppers into 1-in/2.5-cm wide strips.

Toast bread slices on grill over medium-hot coals or broil 4 in/10 cm from heat for 1–2 minutes per side, or until bread is browned.

Arrange bell pepper strips on top of toasted bread. Top with a slice of onion. Drizzle each open sandwich with a few drops of the salad dressing. Top with cheese, cutting cheese slices to fit. Sprinkle olives over sandwiches. Cook over medium-hot coals or broil 4 in/10 cm from heat for about 2 minutes, or until the cheese is melted.

STEP 1

Grilling Bell Peppers

Arrange cored and seeded bell pepper halves, skin-side-down, on the lightly oiled cooking rack of a grill. Grill over medium-hot coals until the skins are evenly charred. Or roast peppers skin-side-up under a preheated broiler.

STEP 2

Steaming Bell Peppers

Immediately after grilling or broiling, remove the charred bell peppers with tongs and place in a paper bag. Close the bag tightly and let stand for at least 10–15 minutes. This allows the steam to loosen the skins.

STEP 3

Removing Skin

Remove the cooled bell peppers from the bag. With a small paring knife, peel off as much of the charred skin as will pull away.

Sichuan Grilled Eggplant and Spinach Salad

Traditionally, the eggplant is steamed for this recipe, but grilling produces a firmer texture and enhances the natural flavor.

INGREDIENTS

6 Asian eggplant (aubergine), each about 6 in/15 cm long, or 1 large globe eggplant, about 1 lb/500 g

Peanut oil, for brushing

SICHUAN SESAME DRESSING

2 tablespoons peanut oil

1 piece ginger root, 1 in/2.5 cm long, peeled and grated

3 cloves garlic, finely minced

½ teaspoon salt

1 teaspoon sugar

¼ cup/2 fl oz/60 ml soy sauce

¼ cup/2 fl oz/60 ml red wine vinegar or balsamic vinegar

1 ½ tablespoons Asian sesame oil

1 teaspoon chili oil

½ cup/4 fl oz/125 ml chicken stock

1 tablespoon sesame seeds

1 lb/500 g fresh spinach

1 tablespoon chopped green (spring) onion

1 tablespoon chopped cilantro (fresh coriander/Chinese parsley)

METHOD FOR MAKING SICHUAN GRILLED EGGPLANT AND SPINACH SALAD

Preparation time 20 minutes
(plus 30 minutes for coals to heat)
Cooking time about 10 minutes
Makes 6 servings

Preheat a gas broiler (grill) to medium-high or prepare a fire in a charcoal grill. If using Asian eggplant, cut lengthwise into slices ¼ in/6 mm thick. If using globe eggplant, cut crosswise into slices ¼ in/6 mm thick. Lightly score the flesh with a large crosshatch pattern. Brush lightly on both sides with peanut oil and grill, turning once, for about 4 minutes, or until the slices are tender, spongy and have light grill marks. Transfer to a plate to cool. Cut into strips ¼ in/6 mm wide and 2 in/5 cm long. Refrigerate, covered, in a bowl.

Warm peanut oil in a small saucepan over medium heat. Add ginger and garlic and cook gently for about 1 minute, or until fragrant but not browned. Stir in salt, sugar, soy sauce, vinegar, sesame and chili oils and simmer for 15 seconds. Stir in chicken stock. Cool.

Toast sesame seeds in a small, dry pan over medium heat for about 3 minutes, or until golden and fragrant.

Carefully stem, wash and dry spinach leaves. Arrange on a platter. Add green onion, cilantro and cooled dressing to eggplant and toss to mix well. Scatter eggplant over the spinach and refrigerate until well chilled. Sprinkle salad with toasted sesame seeds just before serving.

Skewered New Potatoes and Onions

If you cannot find tiny pearl (pickling) onions, peel a white or red (Spanish) onion and cut it into wedges. Do not cook the onion wedges before threading them onto skewers. If using wooden skewers, first soak them in water for 30 minutes to prevent scorching.

INGREDIENTS

VEGETABLES

2 lb/1 kg whole tiny new red potatoes

6 oz/185 g unpeeled pearl (pickling) onions

MARINADE

¼ cup/2 fl oz/60 ml olive oil

2 tablespoons lime or lemon juice

1 tablespoon finely chopped fresh dill or 1 teaspoon dried dillweed

2 cloves garlic, minced

¼ teaspoon salt

¼ teaspoon pepper

Preparation time 15 minutes
(plus 30 minutes for coals to heat)
Marinating time 1 to 2 hours
Cooking time 20 to 25 minutes
Makes 6 servings as an
accompaniment

Prepare potatoes by cutting any large ones in half. Cook potatoes in a large saucepan in a small amount of boiling salted water for 10 minutes; drain. Cook onions in boiling salted water for 5 minutes; drain and rinse in cool water. Trim off stem end of each onion; pop off skins with fingers. Thread potatoes and onions alternately on 6 skewers, each about 12 in/30 cm long. Place in a shallow non-aluminum baking dish.

Combine olive oil, lime or lemon juice, dill or dillweed, garlic, salt and pepper in a screw-top jar. Cover and shake marinade until combined. Pour over vegetable skewers; let stand at room temperature, turning occasionally, for 1–2 hours.

Remove skewers from dish, reserving marinade. Cook skewered vegetables on an uncovered grill directly over medium-hot coals for 10–15 minutes, or until tender. To serve, remove vegetables from skewers and toss with remaining marinade.

Fresh herbs, citrus juice and the smoky flavor of charcoal transform a platter of plain root vegetables.

Grilled Corn with Zesty Cheese Butter

Instead of wrapping corn in foil, enclose it in its own husk and soak well before roasting on the grill. To serve, remove the husks and smear the corn with a peppery cheese spread.

INGREDIENTS

6 cobs of corn

CHEESE BUTTER

3 oz/90 g margarine or butter, softened

1½ oz/45 g shredded sharp Cheddar, Swiss or crumbled blue cheese

¾ oz/25 g finely chopped green (spring) onion

½ teaspoon white wine Worcestershire sauce

¼ teaspoon chili powder

¼ teaspoon pepper

Grilling enhances and deepens corn's sweet delicacy, while a simple seasoned butter spices up the flavor.

Preparation time 25 minutes
(plus 30 minutes for coals to heat)
Cooking time 25 to 50 minutes
Makes 6 servings as an
accompaniment

Pull down husks from corn without removing ends; pull off silk.
Rinse corn; rewrap corn with husks and tie securely with kitchen
string. Soak cobs in water for 15 minutes.

Meanwhile, for cheese butter, combine softened margarine or butter
with cheese, green onion, wine, Worcestershire sauce, chili powder
and pepper in a medium mixing bowl; stir until blended. Cover and
set aside. (Or prepare ahead and chill; let stand 30 minutes to soften
before using.)

Remove corn from water; cook on a preheated, uncovered grill
directly over medium-hot coals, turning frequently, for about
25–35 minutes for tender young corn and 40–50 minutes for
more mature corn, or until kernels are tender. Remove strings and
husks from corn. Serve corn with cheese butter.

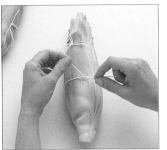

STEP 1

Removing Silk

Strip off the husk almost completely to expose the kernels, but leave the husk attached at the bottom. Pull away the silky inner strands.

STEP 2

Tying the Husk

Once all the silk is removed, pull up the husk to cover the kernels again. Tie securely around in 2 or 3 places with kitchen string.

STEP 3

Soaking

So the corn won't burn on the grill, immerse the cobs of corn in a large bowl of cold water for 15 minutes, or until the husks and strings are thoroughly soaked.

Bruschetta with Tomatoes, Beans and Herbs

The city of Lucca, in Tuscany, is famous for its outstanding olive oil, showcased here in the garlic-scented toast known as bruschetta. Serve it also with marinated roasted bell peppers (capsicums) or other ingredients of your choice.

INGREDIENTS

TOPPING

6 oz/185 g seeded and diced ripe beefsteak tomato

5½ oz/170 g well-drained cannellini beans (freshly cooked or canned)

1¼ oz/37 g seeded and diced cucumber

2 tablespoons thinly sliced green (spring) onion

1 tablespoon fresh oregano leaves or 1½ teaspoons dried oregano

1 tablespoon chopped fresh basil leaves or 1½ teaspoons dried basil

Freshly ground pepper

BRUSCHETTA

8 slices country-style white or wholewheat (wholemeal) bread, each 2½ in/6 cm wide and ½ in/2 cm thick

1 large clove garlic, cut in half

4 teaspoons extra virgin olive oil

Grilling and Broiling

Preparation time 15 minutes
Standing time up to 2 days
Cooking time 5 minutes
Makes 6 servings

Combine all topping ingredients in a bowl, including pepper to taste. Toss well, cover and refrigerate for 2–24 hours to allow the flavors to develop.

Preheat the broiler (grill) or prepare a fire in a charcoal grill. Arrange bread slices on a rack on a broiler or grill pan and toast for 2 minutes. Turn the slices over and brown for 1–2 minutes longer, or until bread is golden brown. Remove from the heat, rub a cut side of the garlic clove over one side of each slice and brush with oil.

Pile equal amounts of topping on the garlic-rubbed side of each bread slice. Transfer bruschetta to a platter and serve immediately.

Grilled Polenta with Grilled-Tomato Sauce

Polenta acquires a crisp crust and a dusky flavor when cooked over coals, and herbed basting oil adds an unusual flavor dimension. Top the polenta with a simply seasoned chunky tomato sauce made with tomatoes that have been charred on the same grill.

INGREDIENTS

SAUCE

6 medium ripe tomatoes

1 tablespoon olive oil

2 green (spring) onions, sliced

2 cloves garlic, minced

½ teaspoon salt

¼ teaspoon pepper

POLENTA

¼ cup/2 fl oz/60 ml olive oil

1 tablespoon finely chopped fresh basil or 1 teaspoon dried basil, crushed

1 tablespoon finely chopped fresh sage or thyme or 1 teaspoon dried sage or thyme, crushed

½ recipe Polenta alla Romana (see *recipe page 48*), chilled

Parmesan cheese, grated

Fresh tomato sauce adds texture and a mild tartness to grilled polenta, which is both grainy, like cornmeal (maize flour), and smooth, like custard.

METHOD FOR MAKING GRILLED POLENTA
WITH GRILLED-TOMATO SAUCE

Preparation time 10 minutes
(plus 30 minutes for coals to heat)
Cooking time about 20 minutes
Makes 4 servings as an
accompaniment

For sauce, place tomatoes on an uncovered grill directly over medium-hot coals. Cook, turning occasionally with tongs, for 5–6 minutes, or until skin is blistered and charred in spots. Remove from grill and cool slightly.

Halve tomatoes, squeeze out and discard seeds; do not peel. Chop tomato flesh. Heat oil in a large frying pan. Add green onion and garlic; cook for 2 minutes. Stir in chopped tomato, salt and pepper. Bring to the boil. Reduce heat, cover and simmer for 5 minutes.

Meanwhile, stir oil with basil and sage or thyme in a small mixing bowl. Cut chilled polenta into 8 slices, each about ½ in/2 cm thick. Brush both sides generously with herb–oil mixture. Cook polenta slices on an uncovered grill directly over medium-hot coals for 6–7 minutes, or until bottoms are golden brown. Brush tops generously with herb–oil mixture, turn and cook for 6–7 minutes longer, or until golden brown.

Arrange polenta on a serving platter; spoon sauce over top. Sprinkle with Parmesan cheese and serve immediately.

Grilled Squash with Brown Sugar Glaze

Light the grill in fall when the gourds come to market.
Besides acorn squash, you can also make this recipe with any
of the small varieties of pumpkin.

INGREDIENTS

3 acorn squash or small
pumpkins, halved (about
1 lb/500 g each)

1 tablespoon cooking oil

2 oz/60 g raisins (optional)

2½ oz/75 g packed brown sugar

Pinch of ground nutmeg

2 tablespoons margarine
or butter

2 tablespoons granola or
chopped nuts

Grill squash or small pumpkins in early fall, when the balmy weather of an Indian summer tempts you to cook outdoors just a few more times.

Preparation time 10 minutes
(plus 30 minutes for coals to heat)
Cooking time 45 to 55 minutes
Makes 6 servings as an
accompaniment

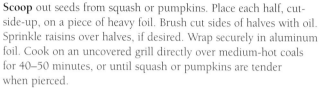

Scoop out seeds from squash or pumpkins. Place each half, cut-side-up, on a piece of heavy foil. Brush cut sides of halves with oil. Sprinkle raisins over halves, if desired. Wrap securely in aluminum foil. Cook on an uncovered grill directly over medium-hot coals for 40–50 minutes, or until squash or pumpkins are tender when pierced.

Combine brown sugar and nutmeg. Unwrap squash or pumpkins on the grill. Sprinkle with brown sugar–nutmeg mixture and dot with margarine or butter. Carefully rewrap and grill for about 5 minutes more, or until brown sugar and butter melt. Sprinkle with granola or nuts.

Broiled Eggplant Moussaka

Three different cheeses flavor this version of Greek moussaka. Choose eggplant (aubergines) that are plump, glossy and heavy for their size. Broil the slices, rather than frying them, to cut down on fat.

INGREDIENTS

2 to 3 fl oz/60 to 80 ml olive oil

1 large red (Spanish) onion, chopped

2 tablespoons plain flour

2 cups/16 fl oz/500 ml milk

½ teaspoon salt

⅛ teaspoon ground nutmeg

2 eggs, lightly beaten

1 large eggplant (aubergine), about 1 lb/500 g, peeled and cut in slices ¼ in/6 mm thick

2 oz/60 g feta cheese, crumbled

4 oz/125 g mild melting cheese, grated

2 tablespoons grated Parmesan cheese

Although moussaka traditionally includes meat, this vegetarian version makes a substantial main course.

Preparation time 30 minutes
Cooking time 50 minutes
Makes 6 to 8 servings as a
main course

Heat 2 tablespoons of oil in an
8-cup/64-fl-oz/2-l saucepan. Add
onion and cook over medium
heat for 3 minutes. Stir in flour
and cook 1 minute; add milk, all
at once. Cook and stir until
thickened and bubbly. Stir in salt
and nutmeg. Stir ½ cup/4 fl oz/
125 ml of the milk mixture into
beaten eggs; gradually stir egg
mixture back into remaining
milk mixture, stirring constantly.
Cover and remove from heat.

Preheat broiler. Arrange
eggplant slices on a large baking

sheet. Brush both sides of slices
with the remaining 2 to
3 tablespoons olive oil. Broil
slices 4 in/10 cm from heat,
turning once, for 8–10 minutes,
or until golden brown. (If all
slices do not fit on baking sheet,
broil half the slices at a time.)

Arrange half the broiled slices in
a greased 8-cup/64-fl-oz/2-l
rectangular baking dish. Spoon
half the milk sauce evenly over
eggplant slices. Sprinkle all the
feta cheese and half the melting
cheese over sauce. Arrange
remaining eggplant slices in a
layer over cheeses; sprinkle with
remaining melting cheese.
Spoon remaining sauce over all;
sprinkle Parmesan cheese on

top. Bake, uncovered, in a
preheated oven, 350°F/180°C/
Gas Mark 4, for 30 minutes, or
until thoroughly heated through.

Serve immediately with dressed
or grilled vegetables of your
choice, or a grilled vegetable
salad (*see recipe page 184*).

Grilled Vegetable Salad

Perfect for cookouts, this hearty salad can be started as soon as the coals warm up,
leaving time for the vegetables to marinate while you cook the rest of the meal.
Alternatively, grill the vegetables the day before—the flavor will improve overnight.

INGREDIENTS

2 red (Spanish) onions, unpeeled

¼ cup/2 fl oz/60 ml red
wine vinegar

1 teaspoon salt, or to taste

½ teaspoon freshly ground
black pepper

1 large clove garlic, minced

3 tablespoons coarsely chopped
fresh oregano or marjoram

⅔ cup/5 fl oz/155 ml olive oil

1 medium or 2 small Japanese
eggplant (aubergines)

1 zucchini (courgette)

1 yellow crookneck squash

1 bulb fennel

1 large bell pepper (capsicum),
seeded, ribs removed and
quartered

Lettuce leaves

Grilling and Broiling

Preparation time 30 minutes
Cooking time 50 minutes
Makes 6 to 8 servings as a main course

Preheat broiler (grill), or prepare fire in a charcoal grill. If using a broiler, place unpeeled onions in a small baking dish and cover with aluminum foil. Place pan in broiler or place

onions directly on the grill rack about 5 in/13 cm from the heat source. Broil or grill, turning every 5–10 minutes, for about 1 hour if using the broiler or 20–30 minutes if using a grill, or until charred on the outside and soft right through. Remove from heat source and cool slightly.

Whisk vinegar with salt, pepper, garlic and oregano or marjoram in a small bowl. Slowly add olive oil, whisking constantly.

Trim ends from the eggplant and squash and any stalk from the fennel and cut all lengthwise into quarters. Place in a bowl with the bell pepper and half the vinaigrette. Toss to mix. Arrange

vegetables on a broiler pan or directly on the grill rack about 5 in/13 cm from the heat source. Broil or grill slowly, turning them so they cook evenly, for about 5–10 minutes for the squash, peppers and eggplant and 15 minutes for the fennel, or until lightly golden and cooked through. Remove from the heat source and set aside to cool slightly.

Peel onions and cut into 2-in/5-cm pieces. Cut remaining vegetables into 2-in/5-cm pieces. Place all in a bowl. Pour over remaining vinaigrette and toss well. Arrange lettuce leaves on individual plates and spoon dressed vegetables on top.

Two Sauces for Grilled and Broiled Vegetables

Peanut Satay Sauce Combine 8 oz/250 g chunky peanut butter in the top of a double boiler with 4 fresh chilies, seeded and sliced, 2 cloves garlic, minced, 2 tablespoons sugar, 1 teaspoon cayenne pepper, 5 tablespoons fresh lime juice, 5 tablespoons dark soy sauce, 3 tablespoons peanut oil and 2 tablespoons water. Cook sauce, stirring until well blended, over water for 5 to 10 minutes. Alternatively, combine ingredients in a bowl, microwave on High for 1½ to 2 minutes and mix well.
Makes about 2½ cups/20 fl oz/625 ml.

Olive Aïoli Process 3 cloves garlic, peeled, with 3 tablespoons puréed Kalamata olives, 1 teaspoon chopped fresh rosemary and ½ cup/4 fl oz/125 ml whole-egg mayonnaise in a food processor until smooth. With motor running, add 2 to 3 tablespoons extra-virgin olive oil through the feed tube, a few drops at a time, until the aïoli is soft and smooth. Add ½ teaspoon fresh lemon juice and process briefly. Keeps for up to 1 week in an airtight jar in the refrigerator.
Makes about ¾ cup/6 fl oz/185 ml.

BAKING

Steps for Baking Vegetables and Grains

Of all the cooking techniques used for vegetables and grains, baking demands the most time but requires the least attention. Once the steps of the recipe are complete and the dish has been put in the oven, you have time to concentrate on the rest of the meal or to relax with a glass of wine before dinner. Success is assured, without the need to hover over a hot grill or smoky wok.

Whether a simple mélange of vegetables coated with oil and roasted, or a complex dish incorporating grains, vegetables and eggs, these preparations emerge from the oven robust and full of flavor, fitting companions for the main dish you have prepared. In many cases, they are substantial enough to be the main course.

On the following pages, you'll see the basic steps for preparing a baked vegetable-and-grain casserole. Because of the variety of recipes in this chapter, some, but not all, of these steps apply to the different dishes ahead. But universal to all baked vegetable and grain recipes is the transformation in flavor that results from a lengthy exposure to the heat of the oven.

BASIC TOOLS FOR BAKING VEGETABLES AND GRAINS

Baking requires ovenproof cookware,
a saucepan for preparing foods to be
baked, a knife to test for doneness and
spoons for stirring, measuring and
transferring food from pan to dish.

saucepan

baking dish

small bowl

knife

tablespoon

measuring
spoons

slotted spoon

Be sure to grease the dish all the way up the sides, or portions of the filling will stick to the dish in ungreased areas.

The coating (here, wheat germ) adds flavor and keeps the filling from sticking to the baking dish.

Don't push the filling around, or it will disturb the coating on the dish.

STEP 1

Greasing the Dish

Dip a paper towel in oil, butter, margarine or shortening. Swirl the towel around the specified baking dish. Apply the fat generously in an even layer on the sides and bottom of the inside of the dish.

STEP 2

Coating the Dish

Some recipes call for sprinkling the dish or pan with breadcrumbs, ground nuts, cheese or wheat germ. Scoop up the ingredient with a spoon. Sprinkle to coat the dish evenly on the sides and bottom.

STEP 3

Spreading the Mixture

Transfer the filling to the prepared dish. With a spoon, spread the filling so that it forms a smooth layer; otherwise it may not flatten out during baking and perhaps will cook unevenly.

The topping adds flavor and turns a golden color when baked.

STEP 4

Topping with Cheese

With a spoon, sprinkle cheese, or any other topping specified, over the filling so that it covers as much of the surface as possible. Don't mound it, or the surface will develop mottled brown areas.

Baked casseroles will cut more easily if rested for a few minutes first.

STEP 5

Testing for Doneness

Just before the specified baking time, open the oven and pull the rack out. Insert a sharp knife near the center. If it comes out clean, the dish is ready; if not, bake a few minutes more. For eggless dishes, bake until hot and bubbly at the edges.

This crustless vegetable-rice entrée epitomizes the delicious potential of baked vegetables and grains. The recipe for Cauliflower, Zucchini and Rice Pie is on page 239.

193

Baked Fennel

Fresh fennel, a native of the Mediterranean, looks a little like celery. It has a light licorice flavor and a celerylike texture. In this recipe, the fennel comes out tender and moist, with its flavor wonderfully mellowed.

INGREDIENTS

2 fennel bulbs, each about 1 lb/500 g

1½ teaspoons extra-virgin olive oil

4 cloves garlic, lightly crushed (optional)

Salt and freshly ground white pepper

Preparation time 10 minutes
Cooking time 20 to 35 minutes
Serves 4 as an accompaniment

Preheat oven to 450°F/230°C/Gas Mark 6.

Trim stem ends and remove any bruised outer leaves from the fennel. Cut each bulb lengthways into sixths; the core portion will hold each wedge intact.

Coat the dull side of a large sheet of aluminum foil with olive oil. Arrange fennel wedges on oiled surface of foil, tuck the garlic, if using, among the wedges and season to taste with salt and white pepper. Fold the foil over, bringing the edges together and folding them over twice to make a double seal. Place on a baking sheet.

Place baking sheet on a rack in the center of the oven and immediately reduce the heat to 400°F/200°C/Gas Mark 5. Bake for 15 minutes. Turn the pouch over and bake for 10–15 minutes longer, or until the fennel is fragrant and tender when pierced. (To test for doneness, remove the pouch from the oven, unfold a corner and pierce fennel with a fork.) Seal and bake for a few more minutes if the fennel is not tender enough.

To serve, remove fennel from pouch and transfer to a warmed serving dish. Serve immediately.

STEP 1

Trimming Fennel

Lay fennel on one flat side on a cutting board and anchor with your hand. With a sharp knife, trim the stalks and feathery leaves to within 1 in/2.5 cm of the bulb.

STEP 2

Slicing Fennel

Using a sharp knife, slice each fennel bulb into quarters or sixths, as called for in the recipe, from top to base. If the recipe calls for slices, take each of the fennel wedges and cut crosswise into slices about ¼ in/6 mm thick.

Carrot and Corn Pudding

Folding is the key to a light, high-rising pudding. The goal is to combine the beaten whites into the heavy purée without deflating the whites. One trick is to mix some of the whites into the purée to lighten it, then fold the rest of the whites into the purée.

INGREDIENTS

3 medium carrots, peeled and finely chopped (about 2½ cups)

1 cup/8 fl oz/250 ml water

1¼ cups/10 fl oz/310 ml half-and-half (half cream), light cream or milk

3 egg yolks

½ teaspoon salt

½ teaspoon sugar

Dash of ground nutmeg

6 oz/185 g fresh or frozen corn kernels or chopped broccoli

2 tablespoons margarine or butter

6 green (spring) onions, sliced

2 tablespoons cornstarch (cornflour)

2 tablespoons chopped fresh parsley

3 egg whites

An airy froth of beaten egg whites adds lightness to this soufflé-like vegetable pudding.

Preparation time 20 minutes
Cooking time 50 to 60 minutes
Serves 6 to 8 as an accompaniment

Combine carrots and water in a medium saucepan. Bring to the boil; reduce heat. Simmer, covered, for 10–12 minutes, or until very tender. Drain. In a blender container or food processor bowl combine cooked carrots, ¼ cup/2 fl oz/60 ml of the half-and-half, 3 egg yolks, salt, sugar and nutmeg. Cover and blend or process until puréed. Set aside.

Cook corn or broccoli in a small saucepan in boiling water until tender, about 4 minutes for corn and 8 minutes for broccoli. Drain. Melt margarine in a large saucepan and cook green onion for 2 minutes. Stir in cornstarch. Add remaining half-and-half, all at once. Cook and stir until mixture is thickened and bubbly. Stir in carrot purée, corn or broccoli and parsley.

Beat egg whites on high speed in a medium mixing bowl with an electric mixer until stiff peaks form (tips stand straight up). Fold a little into carrot mixture to lighten it, then fold rest of egg whites into carrot mixture. Turn into a greased 8-cup/2-qt/2-l rectangular baking dish. Bake in a preheated 325° F/160°C/Gas Mark 3 oven for about 30–35 minutes, or until golden brown and a knife inserted near the center comes out clean. Serve immediately.

STEPS FOR PREPARING CARROT AND CORN PUDDING

STEP 1

Stirring in Purée

Cook the cream sauce until thickened and bubbly. Add carrot purée, corn and parsley. Stir with a wooden spoon until sauce and vegetables are thoroughly blended.

STEP 2

Beating to Stiff Peaks

Put egg whites in the bowl of an electric mixer. Beat at high speed until peaks stand straight up when the beaters are removed.

STEP 3

Folding Together

Cut down through the center of the egg white with the edge of a rubber spatula, come across the bottom of the bowl, then lift up in one smooth motion. Rotate the pan a quarter turn for each fold.

Candied Yams

The dark, orange-fleshed variety of sweet potato commonly known as the yam has been a staple in the southern States since colonial times. This recipe plays on their intrinsic sweetness for its delicious effect.

INGREDIENTS

5 yams or sweet potatoes, unpeeled, about
4 lb/2 kg total weight

TOPPING

1 cup/7 oz/220 g dark brown sugar

4 oz/125 g unsalted butter, at room temperature

2 oz/60 g walnuts or pecans, finely chopped

1 teaspoon pumpkin pie spice

Preparation time 15 minutes
Cooking time about 1¼ hours
Serves 6–8 as an accompaniment

Preheat oven to 425°F/210°C/Gas Mark 5.

Wrap each yam in aluminum foil, pierce all over with a fork and place on a baking sheet. Bake for about 1 hour, or until yams feel tender when pierced with a sharp knife.

Remove yams from oven and reduce oven temperature to 400°F/200°C/Gas Mark 5. Unwrap yams immediately and let cool. Peel yams with your fingers or a sharp knife and slice, crosswise, into 1-in/2.5-cm-thick slices.

For topping, combine brown sugar, butter, walnuts or pecans and spice in a bowl. Using a fork or your fingers, mix until coarse and crumbly.

Lightly butter an 8-in/20-cm-square baking dish. Arrange half the yam slices in a single layer in prepared dish. Sprinkle evenly with half the topping. Arrange remaining yam slices on top and sprinkle with remaining topping. Place baking dish on a baking sheet and bake for 10–15 minutes, or until topping is melted and bubbly. Serve immediately.

About Walnuts and Pecans

While walnuts originated in ancient Persia, pecans are native to the Americas and are closely related to the hickory nut. They were traditionally prized by the Native American peoples. Both nuts are oily and have a high protein and fiber content, so they make a valuable contribution to the vegetarian diet.

Freshness is paramount with both of these nuts, so buy shelled nuts in small quantities from a supplier who turns over the stock frequently. Store in an airtight container in the refrigerator and use quickly. If you buy unshelled nuts, it's all right to buy more at a time, but store them, preferably away from the light, in a cool, dry, airy place. Light tends to make oils oxidize more rapidly and your nuts will become rancid.

Walnuts are usually used unblanched, but if you don't care for the slight bitterness in the brown skin covering the nut itself, and you have lots of patience and spare time, they can be blanched in the following way. Cover shelled nuts with cold water, bring to the boil and simmer for 3 minutes. Remove from the heat and peel nuts, one at a time, with a very sharp knife. Peeled walnuts are usually available in cans from Chinese food stores.

205

Spaghetti Squash with Fresh Tomato Sauce

Spaghetti squash, a bright yellow, football-shaped vegetable, has a pale yellow, stringy flesh that resembles spaghetti when cooked. After baking, run the tines of a fork down the inside of the squash to separate it into strands.

INGREDIENTS

1 spaghetti squash, about 3 lb/1.5 kg

2 lb/1 kg tomatoes

1 tablespoon olive oil or cooking oil

8 green (spring) onions, sliced

1 clove garlic, minced

2 tablespoons chopped fresh basil or 2 teaspoons dried basil, crushed

1 teaspoon salt

1 teaspoon sugar

¼ teaspoon pepper

Transforming tough-skinned spaghetti squash into flavorful golden strands may seem like a culinary parlor trick, but there's no magic to it. The flesh softens into spaghetti-like strings when the squash is cooked.

Preparation time 20 minutes
Cooking time 40 to 50 minutes
Serves 6 as an accompaniment

Halve squash lengthways; scoop out seeds. Place squash, cut-side-down, in a baking dish. With a fork, prick the skin all over. Bake in a preheated 350°C/180°F/Gas Mark 4 oven for 30–40 minutes, or until tender.

Meanwhile, for sauce, fill a large saucepan with water; bring to the boil. Core tomatoes; plunge into boiling water for 30 seconds to loosen skins. Transfer tomatoes to a colander; rinse with cool water. When tomatoes are cool enough to handle, remove skins. Halve peeled tomatoes crosswise. Squeeze out and discard seeds. Chop tomato flesh and set aside.

Heat oil in a large frying pan; cook and stir green onions and garlic for 2 minutes. Add tomatoes, basil, salt, sugar and pepper. Bring to the boil; reduce heat. Simmer, uncovered, for about 5 minutes, or until mixture is of desired consistency. Using a fork, separate the squash pulp into strands and mound on a serving platter. Spoon tomato sauce over squash.

STEPS FOR PREPARING SPAGHETTI SQUASH

STEP 1

Halving Squash

Steady the squash on a folded towel on a cutting board. Ease the blade of a long, sharp knife into one of the ridges. Strike the knife near the bolster with a rubber mallet, or pierce the squash in the center and cut toward each end to split open.

STEP 2

Seeding Squash

Separate the split squash into two halves lengthways. With a large metal spoon, scoop out the seeds but don't remove any of the stringy fibers.

STEP 3

Shredding Squash

After cooking, scrape along the flesh with a fork to loosen the pulp and separate it into strands. Carefully lift the strands and gently tug to loosen them from the hard skin of the squash.

Roasted Red Pepper Timbales

A timbale is a custard mixture baked in an individual mold called a timbale mold. If you do not have these specialized molds, use ¾-cup/6-fl-oz/190-ml custard cups for this recipe. The timbales are baked in a water bath, which ensures that they cook evenly. The technique for roasting and peeling the peppers is given on page 161.

INGREDIENTS

1 cup/8 fl oz/250 ml water

½ cup/3 oz/90 g brown rice

3 large red bell peppers (capsicums), halved

5 eggs

1 cup/8 fl oz/250 ml half-and-half (half cream), light cream or milk

1 tablespoon chopped fresh basil or 1 teaspoon dried basil, crushed

1 tablespoon chopped fresh dill or 1 teaspoon dried dillweed

¾ teaspoon salt

¼ teaspoon pepper

Brown rice adds texture to individual baked custards, and roasted red peppers tint them a soft salmon pink.

Preparation time 20 minutes
Standing time 20 to 30 minutes
Cooking time 1¾ hours
Serves 6 as an accompaniment

Bring water to the boil in a medium saucepan. Add rice, return to the boil, reduce heat, cover and simmer for about 35 minutes, or until rice is tender and water is absorbed. Let stand, covered, for 5 minutes.

Place peppers, cut-side-down, on a foil-lined baking sheet. Bake in a preheated 425°F/210°C/Gas Mark 5 oven for 20–25 minutes, or until skin is bubbly and dark. Place peppers in a brown paper bag; close. Let stand for 20–30 minutes, or until cool enough to handle. Peel skin from peppers. Cut 1 pepper into julienne strips. Place remainder in a blender or food processor. Cover and process until puréed. (You should have about ⅔ cup/5 fl oz/160 ml.) Set aside.

Combine eggs and milk in a medium mixing bowl; whisk until blended. Stir in rice, bell pepper purée, basil, dill, salt and pepper. Place a few bell pepper strips in each of 6 lightly greased ¾-cup/6-fl-oz/190-ml timbale molds or custard cups. Ladle egg mixture evenly into cups; cover tightly with foil. Place in a shallow baking pan on an oven rack. Pour boiling water into pan to a depth of 1 in/2.5 cm. Bake in a preheated 350°F/180°C/Gas Mark 4 oven for 45–50 minutes, or until a knife inserted near the center comes out clean. Remove from water bath; uncover molds and stand for 10 minutes. Run a knife around edges to loosen timbales from molds. Invert onto individual plates. Serve warm.

STEP 1

Filling the Molds

Lightly grease the molds and place a few bell pepper strips in the bottom of each. Using a ladle, distribute the custard mixture evenly among the 6 molds.

STEP 2

Adding Water

Cover molds tightly with foil and set in a shallow baking pan. Place the pan on the middle rack of a preheated 350°F/180°C/Gas Mark 4 oven. Pour boiling water into the pan so the molds are immersed in about 1 in/2.5 cm of hot water.

Baked Eggs in Pastry with Herbs

This stylish variation on shirred (baked) eggs can be put together in a few easy steps.
The pastry can be made up to a week ahead and stored in the refrigerator.
The pans can be lined with pastry the night before for speedy final assembly.

INGREDIENTS

1 quantity savory pastry dough
(see *recipe page 217*)

1 oz/30 g shredded provolone
or similar semi-soft
medium-aged cheese

2 teaspoons mixed chopped fresh
herbs, such as tarragon, chives,
chervil, thyme and/or flat-leaf
(Italian) parsley, in any
combination

8 eggs

¼ cup/2 fl oz/60 ml heavy
(double) cream

2 tablespoons unsalted butter,
cut into pieces

Preparation time
20 minutes
Cooking time about
20 minutes
Serves 4

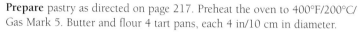

Prepare pastry as directed on page 217. Preheat the oven to 400°F/200°C/Gas Mark 5. Butter and flour 4 tart pans, each 4 in/10 cm in diameter.

Roll out dough on a floured surface to about ⅛ in/3 cm thick and cut out 4 rounds each about 6 in/15 cm in diameter. Carefully transfer rounds to prepared pans, pressing gently against the base and sides of each. Trim off any overhang and, with your thumb and forefinger, crimp the edges attractively. Score bases and sides several times with the tines of a fork. Line with baking paper and weight with pie weights or dried beans.

Bake for 8–10 minutes, or until pale golden brown. Transfer to a wire rack to cool, then remove weights and paper. Reduce oven temperature to 350°F/180°C/Gas Mark 4.

Sprinkle about 1 teaspoon of the cheese over the base of each pastry shell. Combine remaining cheese with herbs in a small bowl. Break 2 eggs into each pastry shell, positioning the yolks side-by-side. Pour 1 tablespoon cream over each pair of eggs, dot the tops with butter, and sprinkle the cheese–herb mixture evenly over the top.

Bake for about 8 minutes, or until eggs are set. Remove from oven and cool for 1 minute. Using a narrow spatula, transfer tarts to individual plates. Serve immediately.

Savory Pastry Dough

Combine 2½ cups/12½ oz/390 g all-purpose (plain) flour with ½ teaspoon salt in a bowl. Add 7½ oz/235 g chilled unsalted butter, cut into pieces. Cut in with your fingers or a pastry blender until mixture looks crumbly and butter is in pea-size pieces.

Add 5 tablespoons/3 fl oz/100 ml ice water and work in very briefly with a wooden spoon to form a rough dough. The less this dough is worked, the more flaky the final pastry will be, so don't try to make the dough a smooth homogeneous ball. Work in unincorporated flour when you are rolling out the dough.

Wrap dough and loose flour particles in plastic wrap (film) and refrigerate for at least 1 hour or up to 1 week before rolling out. Roll out and cut according to directions in the recipe.

Makes enough for 2 pie shells, each 9 in/23 cm in diameter.

Kasha Vegetable Casserole

Kasha, a popular grain in Russian cookery, consists of toasted hulled buckwheat groats.
Look for kasha in the cereal, grain or flour section of your supermarket. You can use
regular buckwheat groats, but they lack the nutty, full flavor of kasha.

INGREDIENTS

1⅓–1½ cups/10½–12 fl oz/
330–375 ml vegetable stock
or water

⅔ cup/4 oz/125 g kasha, rinsed
and drained, or buckwheat groats

2 tablespoons margarine
or butter

4 oz/125 g small broccoli florets

1 large onion, chopped

4 yellow summer (baby) squash
or 2 medium zucchini
(courgettes), diced

2 medium carrots, peeled
and chopped

1 tablespoon chopped fresh basil
or 1 teaspoon dried basil,
crushed

½ teaspoon salt

¼ teaspoon pepper

8 oz/250 g ricotta cheese

1 egg, slightly beaten

4 oz/125 g Monterey Jack or
mozzarella cheese, shredded

In this hearty vegetable casserole, a medley of nutty kasha and sautéed vegetables alternates with rich layers of cheese.

Preparation time 20 minutes
Cooking time 50 to 65 minutes
Serves 6 as a main dish

Combine stock with kasha or buckwheat groats in a medium saucepan. Bring to the boil; reduce heat. Cover and simmer, allowing 25 minutes for kasha and 15 minutes for buckwheat groats, or until all the liquid is absorbed.

Meanwhile, melt margarine or butter in a large frying pan. Add broccoli, onion, squash and carrots. Cook, covered, over medium heat for 5–7 minutes, or until vegetables are crisp-tender. Add kasha or buckwheat groats, basil, salt and pepper. Remove from heat.

Combine ricotta cheese and egg in a small mixing bowl. Spoon half the kasha or buckwheat mixture into a lightly greased 6-cup/1½-qt/ 1.5-l casserole. Spread ricotta mixture evenly over layer in casserole. Spoon remaining kasha or buckwheat mixture over ricotta layer. Cover and bake in a preheated 350°F/180°C/Gas Mark 4 oven for 25–30 minutes, or until heated through. Uncover; sprinkle with shredded cheese. Return to oven for about 3 minutes, or until cheese is melted and golden brown. Serve immediately.

STEP 1

Adding Ricotta Mixture

Grease an ovenproof casserole and fill with half the vegetable mixture. With a spoon, drop dollops of the ricotta cheese mixture over the vegetables.

STEP 2

Spreading Ricotta Mixture

With a rubber spatula, spread the cheese mixture so that it covers the vegetables in an even layer.

Garden Vegetable Strudel

The flaky, golden pastry in this strudel is phyllo, a paper-thin Greek pastry. To keep sheets moist as you're working with them, cover unbuttered stack with plastic wrap (film). For a crisp crust, slash the top of the strudel before baking to allow steam to escape.

INGREDIENTS

6 oz/185 g green beans or yellow wax beans, trimmed and cut into 1-in/2.5-cm lengths

3 to 4 tablespoons olive oil or vegetable oil

8 oz/250 g mushrooms, quartered

10 oz/315 g turnips or rutabagas, peeled and finely chopped

2 medium carrots or parsnips, peeled and chopped

1 large red, yellow or green bell pepper (capsicum), cut into thin strips

1 medium onion or small leek, sliced, or 3 tablespoons chopped green (spring) onion

4 oz/125 g Swiss, Monterey Jack or mozzarella cheese, shredded

1 tablespoon chopped fresh basil or 1 teaspoon dried basil, crushed

2 teaspoons chopped fresh sage or ½ teaspoon ground sage

½ teaspoon salt

¼ teaspoon pepper

6 sheets frozen phyllo pastry (in rectangles about 18 × 14 in/45 × 35 cm), thawed

2 oz/60 g butter or margarine, melted

1 tablespoon grated Parmesan cheese

Each slice of golden strudel reveals a stunning array of colorful, crisp-tender vegetables.

223

Preparation time
20 minutes
Cooking time
40 to 50 minutes
Serves 6 to 8 as an
accompaniment

Cook beans, covered, in a small amount of boiling salted water for
10–12 minutes, or until tender. Drain.

Heat 2 tablespoons olive oil in a 12-in/30-cm frying pan. Cook
mushrooms for 3–5 minutes, or until tender and all liquid is
evaporated. Remove from pan. Add 1 to 2 tablespoons more olive oil;
cook turnips, carrots, pepper and onion for 5–7 minutes, or until
vegetables are crisp-tender. Remove from heat. Stir in beans,
mushrooms, shredded cheese, basil, sage, salt and pepper.

Place 1 sheet of phyllo pastry on a flat surface. Brush with melted
butter. Top with a second piece of phyllo and brush with melted butter.
Repeat with remaining phyllo sheets. Spoon vegetable mixture
lengthwise down the center of pastry, spreading it to within 1 in/2.5 cm
of edges. Fold in short edges about 1 in/2.5 cm; roll dough from long
side, jelly-roll style.

Place roll, seam-side-down, in a 15 x 10 x 1-in/38 x 25 x 2.5-cm
jelly-roll pan. Brush roll with remaining butter; sprinkle with grated
Parmesan cheese. With a sharp knife, make 5 to 7 evenly spaced
diagonal slashes on top of roll. Bake in a preheated 375°F/190°C/Gas
Mark 4 oven for 20–25 minutes, or until golden brown. Let stand for
5 minutes. Cut into 6 to 8 slices and serve.

STEP 1

Layering Phyllo

Top each sheet of butter-coated phyllo with another sheet of pastry (cover unused phyllo with plastic wrap (film) until needed). Brush each sheet with melted butter.

STEP 2

Rolling Strudel

Fold short sides over 1 in/2.5 cm. Roll dough around filling from one long side like a jelly roll.

STEP 3

Slashing

Set roll in a shallow baking pan, brush with butter and sprinkle with cheese. Make 5 to 7 slashes in the top at even intervals.

Roasted Bell Peppers with Melted Cheese

**This classic dish from northern Mexico makes a delightful starter for a winter meal.
Serve with plenty of warm tortillas to scoop up the bubbling mixture.
For a spicier dish, add more fresh chopped chili or chili sauce to taste.**

INGREDIENTS

1 fresh poblano chili, roasted, peeled and seeded

1 red bell pepper (capsicum), roasted, peeled and seeded

1 yellow bell pepper (capsicum), roasted, peeled and seeded

½ white onion, diced

6 oz/185 g Manchego, mozzarella, Monterey Jack or other good melting cheese, grated

2 oz/60 g Cotija, Romano or feta cheese, grated

2 oz/60 g panela, dry cottage or dry ricotta cheese, crumbled

Freshly ground black pepper

12 small flour or corn tortillas, warmed

Prepared salsa, to serve

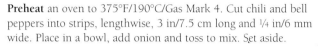

Preparation time 10 minutes
Cooking time about 15 minutes
Serves 6

Preheat an oven to 375°F/190°C/Gas Mark 4. Cut chili and bell peppers into strips, lengthwise, 3 in/7.5 cm long and ¼ in/6 mm wide. Place in a bowl, add onion and toss to mix. Set aside.

Combine cheeses in a separate bowl and mix well. Heat cooking container(s), either a 6-cup/1½-qt/1.5-l earthenware or ovenproof glass baking dish, or 6 similar individual 1-cup/8-fl-oz/250-ml dishes, in the oven for 10 minutes.

Distribute cheeses evenly over the base(s) of dish(es) and return to the oven for 5 minutes. Sprinkle melted cheese with pepper–onion mixture and return to the oven. Bake for 5–7 minutes, or until the cheeses are completely melted and beginning to bubble.

Sprinkle with black pepper and serve immediately with warm tortillas and salsa.

About Chilies

First cultivated by the Mayans some 5000 years ago, the pepper (capsicum) family has been adding fire to cooked dishes around the world since Columbus introduced chilies from their native home. Chilies are now probably the most widely used seasoning of all and there are more than 150 varieties, both sweet and hot. The names can be confusing, since some take different names for fresh and dried forms of the same chili.

Chilies come in many sizes and colors, but all are green before they are ripe. Generally speaking, the smaller the chili, the hotter it is, but there are exceptions. If you are an inexperienced cook, add chili cautiously. You can always add more, but you can't take it out once it's in. Be careful making substitutions, too. Let the quantity called for in the recipe be your guide: if it's a tiny quantity of fresh chili, that chili is likely to be very hot. (The seeds and ribs are especially fiery.)

You can buy chilies fresh, dried, flaked or ground. Store fresh chilies in the refrigerator or, if you have a lot, freeze them or thread them on strings to dry. Just remember their heat becomes more concentrated as they dry. Store dried, flaked or ground chilies in airtight containers in a cool place.

When preparing chilies in significant quantities, always wear gloves and don't touch your eyes or face. As you halve and scrape off the seeds, capsaicin, their fiery ingredient, can spray over your hands and leave them burning painfully for hours.

Baked Vegetable Chips

The fine-slicing blade of a food processor or a mandoline is a great tool for cutting these vegetables. Serve them as you would potato chips: as a snack or as a side dish with a sandwich. Choose either a Mediterranean-style flavor or a dill-based seasoning.

INGREDIENTS

MEDITERRANEAN-STYLE CHIPS

2 tablespoons cooking oil

½ teaspoon garlic salt

¼ teaspoon dried thyme, crushed

¼ teaspoon dried oregano, crushed

⅛ teaspoon pepper

1 lb/500 g root vegetables, such as potatoes or sweet potatoes, parsnips or carrots, peeled and cut into ¼-in/6-mm-thick slices

DILLED CHIPS

2 tablespoons cooking oil

2 cloves garlic, minced

½ teaspoon dried dillweed

⅛ teaspoon salt

1 lb/500 g root vegetables, such as potatoes or sweet potatoes, parsnips or carrots, peeled and cut into ¼-in/6-mm-thick slices

*Unlike the deep-
fried variety, these
oven-baked chips
require a minimum of fat.
The natural goodness of
colorful root vegetables is
enhanced by a choice of
two seasonings.*

Preparation time 15 minutes
Cooking time 20 to 25 minutes
Serves 6 as an accompaniment

For Mediterranean chips, combine oil, garlic salt, thyme, oregano and pepper in a large bowl. Add vegetable slices and toss gently until well coated. Arrange in a single layer on lightly greased baking sheets. Bake in a preheated 350°C/180°C/Gas Mark 4 oven for 20–25 minutes, or until crisp and light golden brown. Serve warm.

For dilled chips, combine oil, garlic, dillweed and salt in a large bowl. Continue as directed above.

Wild Rice-Stuffed Squash

You can also serve this herbed rice stuffing in hollowed-out zucchini (courgette), bell pepper or tomato halves. Just bake for about 20 minutes, or until the vegetables are tender. Vary the stuffing mixture by mixing and matching different kinds of rice.

INGREDIENTS

½ cup/3 oz/90 g wild rice

2 cups/16 fl oz/500 ml water

½ cup/3 oz/90 g brown or long-grain white rice

1 buttercup squash or
2 acorn squash

1 tablespoon cooking oil

1 small red, yellow or green bell pepper (capsicum), chopped

1 medium tomato, chopped

3 tablespoons sliced green onion

1 clove garlic, minced

1 tablespoon chopped
fresh parsley

1 tablespoon chopped fresh oregano or 1 teaspoon dried oregano, crushed

½ teaspoon salt

¼ teaspoon pepper

2 oz/60 g Cheddar or Monterey Jack cheese, shredded

Preparation time 10 minutes
Cooking time 1½ hours
Serves 4 as an accompaniment

Rinse uncooked wild rice; drain. Bring water to the boil in a medium saucepan; stir in drained wild rice and uncooked brown rice (if using). Return to boiling; reduce heat. Cover and simmer for about 40 minutes, or until nearly all the water is absorbed. (If using white rice, add to the wild rice after 20 minutes.)

Halve squash lengthways. Scoop out seeds. Place squash, cut-side-down, on a shallow baking pan. Bake in a preheated 350°C/180°C/Gas Mark 4 oven for 30 minutes. Remove from oven and turn cut-side-up.

Heat oil in a large frying pan. Cook bell pepper, tomato, green onion and garlic in hot oil for 3 minutes. Stir in parsley, oregano, salt and pepper. Drain rice, if necessary; add to frying pan and toss to combine. Spoon mixture into squash cavities, mounding as necessary. Cover; return to oven. Bake for 20–25 minutes more, or until squash is tender and filling is hot.

Uncover; sprinkle with shredded cheese. Return to oven until cheese is melted. Divide each half of buttercup squash into 2 servings.

Golden acorn squash make beautiful, edible cases for a pilaf of seasoned wild and brown rice.

Roasted Onions Stuffed with Cheese

Country cooking at its best, these fragrant onions make both an excellent
appetizer and side dish. The rich, smooth texture of the cheese perfectly
complements the sweetness and crunch of the onions. Roast the
onions slowly to maximize their flavor.

INGREDIENTS

4 medium sweet yellow onions

1 tablespoon cumin seeds

2 oz/60 g Manchego or Monterey
Jack cheese, or other good
melting cheese

4 oz/125 g Cotija, Romano or
other aged cheese, grated

¼ cup/2 fl oz/60 ml sour cream

1 tablespoon balsamic vinegar

3 dashes Tabasco sauce

½ teaspoon salt

½ teaspoon freshly
ground pepper

Preparation time 10 minutes
Cooking time 35 to 40 minutes
Serves 4 as an appetizer or
an accompaniment

Preheat a broiler (griller). Place unpeeled onions in a small baking pan and cover with aluminum foil. Cook about 5 in/13 cm from the heat source, turning every 5–10 minutes, for about 1 hour, or until charred on the outside and soft all the way through. Set aside to cool.

Preheat oven to 375°C/190°C/Gas Mark 4. Peel onions carefully, keeping them intact and discarding the outer charred skin. Cut onions in halves crosswise and, using a finger, remove the centers. Line the bottom of each onion cup with a piece from the center to stop filling leaking out. Chop remaining centers and place in a small bowl.

Toast cumin seeds in a small, dry frying pan over medium heat, shaking pan frequently, for 2–3 minutes, or until seeds are brown and fragrant. Tip seeds onto a cutting board and chop coarsely.

Combine cumin seeds, cheeses, sour cream, vinegar, Tabasco sauce, salt and pepper with onion pulp in the bowl and stir well.

Fill each onion cup with cheese mixture. Place filled onion halves on a baking sheet and bake for 15–20 minutes, or until browned and bubbling. Serve hot.

Cauliflower, Zucchini and Rice Pie

This vegetable pie is like a quiche without a crust. Hearty enough for a main course, it can also be served as a side dish or even a warming breakfast. A layer of wheat germ adds crunch and keeps the custard from sticking to the dish.

INGREDIENTS

About 1 cup/8 fl oz/250 ml water

⅓ cup/2 oz/60 g brown rice or pearl barley

¼ teaspoon salt

2 tablespoons margarine or butter

1 medium zucchini (courgette), shredded

2 oz/60 g finely chopped cauliflower or broccoli

1 onion, chopped

1 tablespoon chopped fresh basil or 1 teaspoon dried basil, crushed

3 eggs, beaten

1½ cups/12 fl oz/175 ml half-and-half (half cream), light cream or milk

2½ oz/75 g Parmesan or Romano cheese, grated

1 tablespoon toasted wheat germ

Preparation time 20 minutes
Cooking time 1 to 1½ hours
Serves 4 as a main course
or 6 as an accompaniment

Bring ⅔ cup/5 fl oz/160 ml water to the boil in a medium saucepan for white or brown rice, or use 1 cup/8 fl oz/250 ml water for barley. Add uncooked rice or barley and salt. Return to the boil; reduce heat. Cover and simmer, allowing 15 minutes for long-grain rice, 35 minutes for brown rice, and 45 minutes for barley, or until grains are tender. Remove from heat. Let stand, covered, for 5 minutes.

Heat margarine in a medium saucepan and cook zucchini, cauliflower, onion and basil, stirring, for 3–5 minutes, or until vegetables are tender but not brown. Stir in cooked rice, eggs, half-and-half and 2 tablespoons of the cheese.

Generously grease a 9-in/22-cm pie plate or quiche dish. Sprinkle evenly with wheat germ. Turn grain mixture into prepared pie plate. Sprinkle with the remaining cheese and bake, uncovered, in a preheated 350°C/180°C/Gas Mark 4 oven for 30–35 minutes, or until a knife inserted near the center comes out clean. Let stand for 10 minutes before cutting into wedges.

Bake this vegetable–rice pie in a rustic stoneware dish that you can bring to the table. The wedges will cut neatly, even without a crust.

Swiss Chard Empanadas

The Mexican version of a turnover, empanadas can be stuffed with all kinds of
vegetables, including squash, mushrooms and the chard used here. Use plenty of chard
and season it well. Make empanadas in large batches and store, well wrapped, in the
freezer. They will keep well for several weeks.

INGREDIENTS

PASTRY

2 cups/10 oz/315 g all-purpose (plain) flour

4 oz/125 g lard or unsalted butter, chilled

2½ tablespoons unsalted butter, chilled

½ teaspoon salt

About ⅓ cup/2½ fl oz/80 ml ice water

SWISS CHARD FILLING

2 tablespoons olive oil

1 large white onion, peeled and diced

1lb/500 g Swiss chard (silverbeet), trimmed, leaves cut into small pieces and stems cut into about ½-in/1-cm dice

1 oz/30 g Manchego or Monterey Jack cheese or other good melting cheese

3 oz/90 g Cotija, Romano or Parmesan cheese

Dash of lime juice

About ½ teaspoon salt

Freshly cracked pepper

1 egg, beaten, for glaze

Preparation time
30 minutes
Cooking time
45 to 50 minutes
Serves 6

Combine flour, lard, butter and salt in a bowl. Mix lightly with your fingers until mixture forms pea-size pieces. Using a fork, stir in the ice water, a little at a time, until a dough forms. Knead lightly until dough comes together in a ball. Wrap in plastic wrap (film) and refrigerate for 1–12 hours.

Heat olive oil over medium heat in a large frying pan. Add onion and cook for 7–10 minutes, or until onion is golden and translucent. Add chard stems and cook for 1–2 minutes. Add chard leaves and cook for 3–4 minutes, or until tender. Turn into a bowl and cool. Add cheeses and lime juice, mix well and season to taste.

To assemble empanadas, roll out dough on a lightly floured board to a thickness of ⅛ in/3 mm. Cut out 12 rounds 3 in/7.5 cm in diameter. Place about 2 tablespoons of filling on one half of each round, leaving a border about ½ in/1 cm wide. Dampen pastry edges with beaten egg, fold over to enclose filling and seal by pressing edges firmly with the tines of a fork. Cover and refrigerate for at least 30 minutes.

Preheat oven to 350°C/180°C/Gas Mark 4. Arrange empanadas on a baking sheet, brush tops with egg glaze and sprinkle with cracked pepper. Cut 2 slits in each so steam can escape and bake for 30 minutes, or until golden. Transfer to a wire rack to cool. Serve warm or at room temperature.

Empanada Filling Variations

Nearly every cuisine includes a version of the delicious empanada, which hails from South and Central American countries, so the range of possible fillings is limited only by your imagination. Here are a few to set you on the path of discovering endless delicious variations.

Spinach and Ricotta Heat a little olive oil in a frying pan and cook 8 oz/250 g chopped spinach over low heat for about 5 minutes, or until it is soft and wilted. Drain well and combine with 8 oz/250 g ricotta or cottage cheese and 3 chopped green (spring) onions.

Mushroom and Goat Cheese Heat a little butter or olive oil in a frying pan and cook 8 oz/250 g peeled mushrooms over low heat for about 8 minutes, or until softened. Drain well, reserving pan juices. Chop mushrooms and combine in a bowl with 4 oz/125 g goat cheese or soft curd cheese, a dash of lemon juice, 2 oz/60 g soft breadcrumbs and 1 tablespoon finely chopped parsley. Moisten with enough of the reserved pan juices to achieve a firm, but not too wet, consistency.

Ratatouille and Basil Heat a little olive oil in a frying pan and cook 4 oz/125 g chopped onion for about 5 minutes, or until golden and translucent. Add 4 oz/125 g chopped tomato, 4 oz/125 g chopped celery, including leaves, and 4 oz/125 g chopped zucchini (courgette). Cook, uncovered, for about 10 minutes, or until flavors are blended, vegetables are soft and most of the liquid has evaporated. Cool. Add 2 tablespoons chopped basil and enough soft breadcrumbs to achieve a firm, but not too wet, consistency.

Baked Peanut and Rice Pilaf

Use any peanuts you like, roasted or raw, skinned or unskinned, salted
or unsalted. Just be sure they are fresh and crunchy. Buy from a store
that turns over its stock regularly. Hoisin sauce is available in
the Asian food section of supermarkets or in Asian markets.

INGREDIENTS

1 tablespoon olive oil

1 onion, chopped

1 cup/7 oz/220 g brown or white long-grain rice, or wild rice rinsed and drained

2 tablespoons hoisin sauce

1 tablespoon soy sauce

⅛ to ¼ teaspoon crushed red pepper flakes (cayenne pepper)

2 cups/16 fl oz/500 ml water

¼ teaspoon salt

8 oz/250 g fresh or thawed frozen peas

2½ oz/75 g peanuts

Hoisin sauce, an Asian condiment, gives this pilaf a sweet, slightly spicy flavor. Peas and peanuts are a last-minute addition, so they will stay crisp.

Preparation time 12 minutes
Cooking time 25 to 45 minutes
Serves 4 as an accompaniment

Heat oil in a large ovenproof frying pan. (If you don't have an ovenproof frying pan, use an ordinary frying pan and transfer the rice mixture to an 8-cup/2-qt/2-l casserole when it is time to cover and bake.) Add onion and cook for 2 minutes. Add rice, hoisin sauce, soy sauce and red pepper flakes; stir until combined. Add water and salt and bring to the boil.

Cover and bake in a preheated 350°C/180°C/Gas Mark 4 oven, allowing 35 minutes for brown rice, 20 minutes for white rice and 40 minutes for wild rice, or until rice is tender and liquid is absorbed. Stir in peas and peanuts 10 minutes before rice is done, cover again and continue to bake.

About Pilafs

Although known by different names in many countries, the basic pilaf is easily recognized, whether baked or cooked on a stovetop or grill (barbecue). It is based on a grain or combination of grains with infinite variations in its possible ingredients and spicing. The spicings favored in many parts of the world include cinnamon sticks, cardamom pods, cloves and saffron threads. Almonds, cashews and other nuts are often incorporated to create a nutritious one-pot dish that is full of flavor and variety.

Start by cooking 1 chopped onion in 1 tablespoon olive oil for 2 minutes. Add 1 cup/7 oz/220 g (total weight) rice, barley and/or lentils, alone or in any combination you like. Add 2 cups/16 fl oz/ 500 ml (total quantity) water or vegetable stock and return to the boil. If cooking in the oven, transfer to an 8-cup/2-qt/2-l casserole and stir through a selection of vegetables and fruits. Add slower-cooking ingredients first, such as celery, carrots, parsnip, chopped tomatoes and fruits such as apple, apricots (especially dried), prunes, raisins, sultanas and currants.

Bake in a preheated 350°C/180°C/Gas Mark 4 oven for 35–40 minutes, or until grain is tender and liquid is absorbed. Stir in nuts and quick-cooking vegetables such as mushroom, zucchini (courgette), broccoli or cauliflower florets and peas 10 minutes before rice is done; cover again and continue to bake. If desired, sprinkle pilaf with your choice of herb before serving.

SALADS AND SOUPS

Steps for Making Salads

Glorious concoctions, salads are artful jumbles that showcase vegetables at their most vibrant. They assume many roles in a meal: as introduction, as accompaniment and as a palate-cleansing intermezzo. And during warm weather, when only something light will satisfy, salads often take center stage as the main course.

Lettuce is the most familiar ingredient in the salad bowl. A marvelous salad can be constructed from just one variety if all the components are carefully chosen, as in a basic green salad with a tart vinaigrette (see pages 254–55).

Or mix a variety of your favorite greens for a change of pace.

Other salads are more complex, with lettuce a minor player or absent. Regardless of the ingredients you choose, a velvety dressing ties it all together. Use only the finest ingredients: flavorful oils and quality vinegars, fresh herbs and select seasonings. Experiment to find ones that please you; well-stocked supermarkets and specialty stores now offer condiments in a huge and exciting variety. Be sure that salad vegetables are washed and thoroughly dried, so that excess moisture doesn't dilute the dressing.

BASIC TOOLS FOR MAKING SALADS AND SOUPS

The best salad bowls are wide and shallow, so the greens can be tossed bottom to top with long-handled servers. Use a cup, bowl and fork to prepare the dressings.

measuring cup

salad bowl

small bowl

fork

salad servers

Discard any leaves that are wilted or damaged by insects.

Alternatively, dry greens in a salad spinner.

If not using immediately, refrigerate greens in a plastic bag lined with paper towels.

STEP 1

Rinsing Lettuce

Fill the sink with enough water that you can move the leaves gently about. Tear leaves from the head and drop in the water. Swish greens around in the water with your hands so dirt or grit is rinsed away.

STEP 2

Drying Lettuce

Set leaves on layers of paper towels. Gently, but thoroughly, pat them with more towels to remove all moisture, including any hidden in their creases. Replace sodden towels with dry ones when necessary.

STEP 3

Tearing Lettuce

Have a salad bowl ready. With your hands, tear the dried leaves into bite-sized pieces (or the size specified in the recipe). Drop into the bowl. If the leaves are small, they can be used whole.

You can also combine dressing ingredients in a glass jar with a screw-top lid, as shown on page 259.

Don't add the oil too quickly, or the dressing will become thin.

Dress the salad just before serving, or it will become soggy and wilted.

STEP 4

Whisking Vinegar
Place 1 tablespoon wine vinegar in a small bowl. Add ½ teaspoon Dijon mustard and ⅛ teaspoon salt. Beat vigorously with a fork until they blend into a homogeneous mixture.

STEP 5

Incorporating Oil
Pour 3 tablespoons extra-virgin olive oil, in a thin stream, into the vinegar mixture. Whisk constantly with a fork as you pour so the mixture thickens and emulsifies.

STEP 6

Tossing Salad
Pour dressing over greens. With your hands or salad servers, gently lift and flip the layers so they turn over. Repeat lifting and tossing until all the greens are coated with a thin, glistening film of dressing.

Four-Green Salad with Toasted-Walnut Dressing

Toss together romaine (cos), red leaf lettuce, watercress and Belgian endive (witloof for an extra-special green salad. Substitute 6 cups of packaged premixed greens if time is short.

INGREDIENTS

DRESSING

¼ cup/2 fl oz/60 ml olive oil or vegetable oil

1 oz/30 g toasted coarsely chopped walnuts or pecans

2 tablespoons raspberry or white wine vinegar

2 teaspoons chopped fresh chives

1 teaspoon sugar

¼ teaspoon salt

⅛ teaspoon pepper

SALAD

2 cups torn romaine (cos) lettuce leaves

2 cups torn red leaf lettuce or spinach leaves

1 cup watercress sprigs

1 head Belgian endive (witloof), sliced, or 1 cup torn curly endive or radicchio (about 3 oz/90 g)

A medley of greens dressed in an exotic walnut vinaigrette demonstrates how artful a monochromatic salad can be.

Preparation time 15 minutes
Serves 4 to 5 as an accompaniment

Combine oil for dressing with walnuts, vinegar, chives, sugar, salt and pepper in a screw-top jar. Cover and shake well to mix. Set aside.

Toss lettuce in a salad bowl with spinach, watercress and endive or radicchio. Shake dressing just before using; drizzle over salad and toss gently to coat. Pass any remaining dressing with salad.

STEP 1

Toasting Nuts
Spread nuts in a metal pie tin. Bake in a preheated 350°F/180°C/Gas Mark 4 oven for 5–10 minutes, or until lightly browned. Stir once or twice so the nuts brown evenly.

STEP 2

Snipping Chives
Hold the chives over a bowl. Using kitchen scissors, snip off little sections about ¼ in/6 mm long.

STEP 3

Blending Dressing
Place all ingredients in a small glass jar with a screw-top lid. Secure the lid and shake vigorously until the ingredients thicken and emulsify.

Caesar Salad

Although every chef puts a personal twist on this famous salad, the key elements remain constant: crisp romaine (cos) lettuce, a tangy vinaigrette and crunchy homemade croutons. This dressing omits the original coddled egg and anchovies.

INGREDIENTS

CROUTONS

4 slices day-old French or Italian bread (each slice about 4 × 2½ in/10 × 6 cm), cut about ¾ in/2 cm thick

¼ cup/2 fl oz/60 ml olive oil

1 clove garlic, minced

Salt

SALAD

1 head romaine (cos) lettuce, washed, drained and torn into bite-size pieces

2 tablespoons mayonnaise

1 tablespoon fresh lemon juice

¼ teaspoon Worcestershire sauce

¼ teaspoon Dijon mustard

¼ teaspoon coarsely ground black pepper

¼ cup/2 fl oz/60 ml extra-virgin olive oil

1½ oz/45 g Parmesan cheese, grated

Most stories credit Caesar Cardini, a restaurateur in Tijuana, Mexico, with concocting this international favorite in the 1920s.

Preparation time 20 minutes
Cooking time 3 minutes
Serves 4 to 6

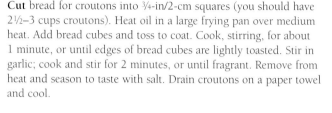

Cut bread for croutons into ¾-in/2-cm squares (you should have 2½–3 cups croutons). Heat oil in a large frying pan over medium heat. Add bread cubes and toss to coat. Cook, stirring, for about 1 minute, or until edges of bread cubes are lightly toasted. Stir in garlic; cook and stir for 2 minutes, or until fragrant. Remove from heat and season to taste with salt. Drain croutons on a paper towel and cool.

Place lettuce for salad in a large salad bowl. In a small mixing bowl, combine mayonnaise, lemon juice, Worcestershire sauce, mustard and pepper until well blended. Whisk in olive oil. Pour dressing over lettuce and toss well. Add croutons and cheese and toss again. Season to taste with salt.

STEP 1

Cutting Bread

Using a serrated bread knife, slice a day-old French or Italian loaf into ¾-in/2-cm-thick slices. Then cut each slice into ¾-in/2-cm-wide strips, but don't separate them. Cut the strips crosswise, creating ¾-in/2-cm-square croutons.

STEP 2

Toasting Croutons

Heat oil in a frying pan and toss croutons, stirring, for about 1 minute. Add garlic and cook for 2 minutes longer, or until croutons are crunchy and slightly golden around the edges.

Vegetable Salad with Spicy Peanut Dressing

Vegetables such as broccoli or cauliflower can be used in place of those called for here, if you prefer. Garnish with hard-boiled eggs cut into wedges and commercially prepared fried onion flakes for added crunch.

INGREDIENTS

SPICY PEANUT DRESSING

1 oz/30 g tamarind pulp

½ cup/4 fl oz/125 ml boiling water, plus extra as needed

2 small, fresh red chilies

1 piece ginger root, 1 in/2.5 cm long, peeled and chopped

1 stalk lemongrass, tender white heart section only

2 cloves garlic

2 shallots, cut in fourths

1 teaspoon salt

1 cup/8 fl oz/250 ml coconut milk

1 tablespoon palm sugar or brown sugar

1½ tablespoons sweet, dark soy sauce

2½ oz/75 g chunky peanut butter

1 tablespoon fresh lemon juice

INGREDIENTS (*continued*)

SALAD

4 small new potatoes

1 lb/500 g spinach

8 oz/250 g bean sprouts

2 carrots, peeled and sliced

6 oz/185 g green beans, cut into
2-in/5-cm lengths

6 oz/185 g shredded cabbage

8 oz/250 g asparagus, cut into
3-in/8-cm lengths

1 cucumber, cut into
½-in/1-cm cubes

Hard-boiled eggs, cut into
segments, for garnish (optional)

Preparation time
about 30 minutes
Cooking time
about 45 minutes
Serves 6

Prepare dressing first. Soak tamarind pulp in boiling water for 15 minutes. Mash with the back of a spoon to help disperse the pulp. Pour through a fine-mesh strainer, pressing against the pulp to extract as much liquid as possible. Discard pulp; reserve liquid.

Seed chilies and process to a smooth paste in a food processor with ginger, lemongrass, garlic, shallots and salt. Transfer to a saucepan and add coconut milk, palm sugar, soy sauce, tamarind liquid and peanut butter. Bring to the boil. Reduce heat and simmer, stirring frequently, for about 15 minutes, or until creamy and fragrant. Add lemon juice and cook for 1 minute longer. Set aside. Just before serving, thin to the consistency of a salad dressing with boiling water.

To prepare salad, bring 2 large pots of water to the boil. In one, cook potatoes for about 20 minutes, or until tender; drain, cool and cut into wedges. In the other pot, parboil your chosen vegetables, separately, refresh under cold water and drain. Allow 5 seconds for spinach; 10 seconds for bean sprouts; 8 minutes for carrots; 1 minute for shredded cabbage; and 3 minutes for asparagus. (Vegetables should retain plenty of crunch.) Arrange vegetables on individual plates. Pour dressing over, garnish with egg segments, if desired, and serve.

Jícama and Blood Orange Salad

Jícama sprinkled with chili powder is eaten as a snack throughout Mexico.
In some parts this crisp white-fleshed root vegetable is teamed with fruit, such as the
blood oranges used here, to make an unusual salad.

INGREDIENTS

1 jícama, about 12 oz/375 g

3 blood oranges

1 papaya, mango or pineapple

1 small red (Spanish) onion, thinly sliced

1 teaspoon sea salt

¼ dried habanero chili, seeded and ground to a powder, or red

pepper flakes (cayenne pepper) to taste (optional)

¼ cup/2 fl oz/60 ml olive oil

Juice of 1 lime

1 bunch fresh cilantro (fresh coriander/Chinese parsley), leaves only

1 bunch fresh mint, leaves only

Preparation time about 30 minutes
Standing time 2 hours
Serves 4 to 6 as an accompaniment

Using a paring knife, peel jícama, removing the fibrous layer just beneath the skin. Slice flesh thinly, then cut into thin strips 2 in/5 cm long and ¼ in/6 mm thick. Place in a large bowl.

Using a sharp knife, cut a slice off the top and bottom of each orange. Working with 1 orange at a time, place upright on a board and cut away the peel and any white membrane. Holding orange over the bowl containing the jícama, cut along either side of each segment to free it, letting juice and skinless segments fall into the bowl. Squeeze any juice from remains of the orange and discard core. (If using papaya, halve lengthways, remove seeds and peel. If using mango, peel and remove pit. If using pineapple, remove skin and tough core. Cut fruit into small dice and add to jícama strips.)

Add onion, salt, chili, olive oil, lime juice, cilantro (fresh coriander/Chinese parsley) and mint and toss salad gently to mix. Cover and refrigerate for 2 hours before serving.

Salad Leaves

Here are just a few of the wonderful selection of salad leaves you can mix or match to create fresh-tasting salads with a variety of colors and textures.

butter lettuce

mignonette lettuce

watercress

arugula (rocket)

radicchio

chicory (curly endive)

French lettuce

spinach

Choose-a-Cabbage Slaw

Use either red or green cabbage or a mixture of both for this colorful salad.
Add another splash of color with a rainbow of bell peppers (capsicum),
yellow squash or radishes.

INGREDIENTS

DRESSING

¼ cup/2 fl oz/60 ml extra-virgin olive oil

2 tablespoons cider vinegar, white wine vinegar or lemon juice

2 tablespoons mayonnaise or salad dressing

2 teaspoons sugar

¼ teaspoon salt

¼ teaspoon pepper

SALAD

About 3 cups shredded green or red cabbage, or a mixture

About 1 cup shredded peeled carrots, zucchini or yellow summer squash

About 1 cup shredded white or red radish or julienne-cut peeled cucumber, red or yellow bell pepper (capsicum), celery or peeled jícama

Cabbage leaves (optional)

Shreds of colorful vegetables mingle in this creamy, casual salad.

Preparation time 20 minutes
Cooking time 5 minutes
Serves 6 to 8 as an accompaniment

Whisk oil in a small mixing bowl with vinegar, mayonnaise, sugar, salt and pepper. Set aside.

For salad, toss shredded cabbage in a large salad bowl with whatever shredded and julienne-cut vegetables you are using. Add salad dressing; toss gently to coat. Turn into a salad bowl lined with cabbage leaves, if desired. Serve at once or cover and chill for up to 24 hours.

STEP 1

Coring Cabbage

Halve cabbage. With a sharp knife, cut down both sides of the white core at an angle to cut out the core in a triangular wedge.

STEP 2

Shredding Cabbage

Divide cabbage halves into 2 pieces. Place one cut side on the cutting board and anchor the wedge with your hand. Using a sharp knife, slice thinly. The slices will separate into thin shreds. This technique can also be used for lettuce.

Vegetable Antipasto Salad

Cover and chill the leftover marinade to use as a salad dressing or as a marinade another time. It can be stored in the refrigerator for up to a week.

INGREDIENTS

SALAD

About 4 oz/125 g whole green beans and/or sugar snap peas

8 baby carrots or turnips, peeled

1 large red, yellow or orange bell pepper (capsicum), cut into strips about ½ in/1 cm wide

About 4 oz/125 g broccoli or cauliflower florets

1 small red onion, cut into thin wedges

3 oz/90 g mushrooms, quartered

3 oz/90 g pitted ripe olives

Lettuce leaves, for garnish (optional)

MARINADE

1 cup/8 fl oz/250 ml white wine vinegar

⅔ cup/5 fl oz/160 ml olive oil or vegetable oil

1 tablespoon capers, drained

1 tablespoon sugar

1 teaspoon dried Italian seasoning, crushed

1½ teaspoons chopped fresh dill or ½ teaspoon dried dillweed, crushed

½ teaspoon salt

¼ teaspoon pepper

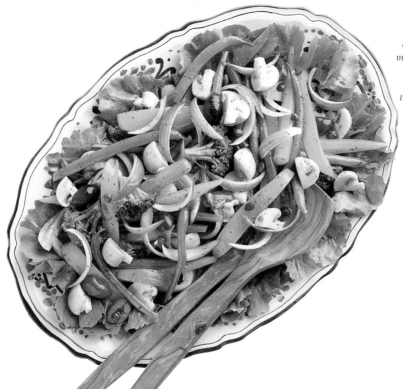

Easily prepared ahead, this lively marinated salad is a perfect starter when the rest of the menu requires last-minute preparation.

METHOD FOR MAKING VEGETABLE ANTIPASTO SALAD

Preparation time about 15 minutes
Cooking time 8 minutes
Chilling time 2 to 24 hours
Serves 8 as an appetizer
or an accompaniment

Steam beans, if using, in a steamer basket over boiling water, covered, for 5 minutes. Add sugar snap peas, if using, baby vegetables, bell pepper and broccoli florets; cover and steam for 3 minutes. Remove steamer from pan; rinse vegetables in cold water. Drain well. In a non-aluminum bowl combine steamed vegetables, onion, mushrooms and olives.

Combine vinegar for marinade in a screw-top jar with oil, capers, sugar, Italian seasoning, dill, salt and pepper. Cover and shake well to mix. Pour mixture over vegetables, stirring to coat. Cover and chill for 2–24 hours.

Drain vegetables, reserving marinade. Serve on a platter lined with lettuce leaves, if desired.

Avocado and Tomatillo Salad

This delightful salad highlights contrasts in textures—the rich creaminess of avocado against the crispness of the tomatillos and the crunchiness of the croutons. Choose ripe avocados that are firm enough to hold up during tossing.

INGREDIENTS

½ cup/4 fl oz/125 ml olive oil

⅓ loaf crusty French, Italian or sourdough bread, cut into ¾-in/2-cm cubes

Salt and freshly ground pepper

2 ripe avocados, pitted, peeled and cut into ¾-in/2-cm cubes

12 oz/375 g red or yellow cherry tomatoes, or a mixture, halved

2 bunches cilantro (fresh coriander/Chinese parsley) leaves only

5 tomatillos, husked and quartered

1 tablespoon fresh lime juice

2 tablespoons white or white wine vinegar

Lettuce leaves

6 green (spring) onions, thinly sliced

Preparation time about 15 minutes
Cooking time 15 minutes
Serves 4 to 6 as an accompaniment

Heat half the olive oil in a frying pan over medium heat. Add bread cubes and shake pan to coat the bread lightly all over. Sprinkle with salt and papper to taste, reduce heat and toast, shaking pan occasionally, for about 15 minutes, or until croutons are crisp and golden brown all over.

Combine avocados, cherry tomatoes and cilantro leaves in a bowl. Process tomatillos with lime juice, vinegar, remaining oil and salt and pepper to taste in a food processor fitted with a metal blade until dressing is smooth.

Pour dressing over avocado mixture and begin to toss lightly. When almost fully mixed, add croutons and toss again.

Line a platter or individual salad bowls with lettuce leaves and spoon salad on top. Garnish with green onions and serve immediately.

In the Soup

Whether your goal is a chunky concoction, a creamed soup, or a clear, elegant reduced stock with ravioli afloat, it's amazing how a few vegetables can be transformed into something fabulous. The basics are aromatics, such as onions, garlic, celery and carrots, fried to a golden brown in good olive oil. Then you must add good stock, either bought or homemade but the best you can muster, and almost any vegetable you can think of. Try peas or spinach with coconut cream, leek and potato with a topping of cheese, or pumpkin with a dash of garam masala. If you intend to purée the soup, cut your vegetables into smallish pieces so that they will cook quickly. You can have this type of soup cooked and on the table in not much longer than it would take you to open a can. Serve simply with fresh crusty bread.

Slower-cooked types of soup, filled with beans and other good things, can be simmering away on the stove, filling the house with wonderful aromas, while you are busy doing other things. Start in the same way, with the aromatics, but give beans plenty of time to cook before adding all the vegetables. You don't want the soup to turn into mush, so vegetables should retain their shape and texture.

For a clear soup or consommé, reduce and strain stock with plenty of flavor until it is clear and intense. For a bit of added drama, cook some vegetarian ravioli in a separate pot of boiling salted water, following the directions on the package. Remove with a slotted spoon and slip a few ravioli into each bowl of consommé as you serve.

Pinto Bean Soup with Fresh Salsa

Despite its creamy taste, this simply prepared soup is surprisingly low in fat.
It's a good way to use up leftover beans and substantial enough to be the perfect
antidote to cold winter days.

INGREDIENTS

10½ oz/330 g dried pinto beans

7 cups/56 fl oz/1.75 l water

¼ cup/2 fl oz/60 ml vegetable oil

2 yellow onions, sliced

1 teaspoon salt

½ teaspoon freshly
ground pepper

4 cloves garlic, minced

6 cups/48 fl oz/1.5 l vegetable
stock or water

SALSA

3 ripe plum (Roma) tomatoes,
diced

½ small red (Spanish) onion,
finely chopped

3 tablespoons coarsely chopped
cilantro (fresh coriander/Chinese
parsley) leaves

Juice of 1 lime

Salt and freshly ground pepper

Sour cream, to serve (optional)

Preparation time about 30 minutes
Cooking time 2 hours
Serves 6 as an accompaniment

Sort through beans and discard any stones or broken or misshapen beans. Rinse well. Place beans in a large saucepan, add water and bring to the boil. Reduce heat and simmer, covered, for about 1½ hours, or until the smallest bean is cooked through and creamy inside. Remove from the heat and set aside.

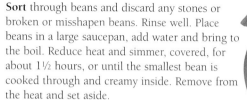

Heat oil in a large saucepan over medium heat and cook onion for about 10 minutes, or until lightly browned and translucent. Add salt, pepper and garlic and cook for 1–2 minutes more. Add beans, including their liquid, and stock. Bring to the boil, reduce heat and simmer, uncovered, stirring occasionally, for 20–30 minutes, or until the beans start to break apart. Remove from the heat and leave to cool slightly.

Meanwhile, make the salsa. Combine tomatoes in a bowl with onion, cilantro and lime juice and season to taste. Refrigerate, covered, until serving time.

Working in batches, transfer bean mixture to a blender and purée until smooth. Transfer purée to a clean saucepan and reheat over low heat, stirring frequently, until hot. (Watch carefully as the soup is likely to scorch on the bottom of the saucepan.)

Ladle soup into warmed bowls and top each with a spoonful of both salsa and sour cream.

Chestnut and Celery Soup

During the winter months, hot roasted chestnuts are cooked on charcoal braziers and sold on the boulevards of Paris. This rich soup is a popular first course over the Christmas and New Year holiday season.

INGREDIENTS

1 lb/500 g prepared unsweetened chestnut purée or 1½ lb/750 g fresh chestnuts

4 oz/125 g unsalted butter

2 white onions, chopped

3 stalks celery, coarsely chopped

1 large russet potato, peeled and coarsely chopped

6 cups/48 fl oz/1.5 l vegetable stock or water

2 cups/16 fl oz/500 ml heavy (double) cream

2 teaspoons salt, or to taste

1 teaspoon ground white pepper

Cooking time about 50 minutes
Serves 6 to 8

If you are using fresh chestnuts, preheat the oven to 400°F/200°C/ Gas Mark 5. Using a sharp knife, cut an X on the flat side of each chestnut. Spread them in a shallow pan and roast for 25–30 minutes, or until chestnuts feel tender when pressed and the shells have curled where they were cut. Remove from the oven and, using a small sharp knife, remove shells and furry skin directly under them. (Chestnuts are easiest to peel while still warm.) Set aside.

Melt butter in a large saucepan over medium heat. Cook onion and celery for about 5 minutes, or until golden and softened.

Add chestnut purée or roasted nut meat, potato, stock and cream and bring to the boil. Reduce heat, season to taste and simmer, uncovered, for about 1 hour, or until soup has thickened slightly.

Working in batches, process soup on high speed in a food processor until smooth and creamy. Transfer to a clean saucepan and reheat over medium heat. Adjust seasoning and ladle into warmed bowls. Serve immediately.

About Chestnuts

Equally at home in sweet and savory dishes, the versatile chestnut was once a staple food, used for grinding into a flour long before grains and potatoes took over that role. Chestnuts must be boiled or roasted before they can be eaten and, of course, encouraged to shuck off that troublesome and reluctant shell. Chestnuts with shells on will yield about half of the original weight when shelled. It is possible to buy shelled chestnut meat frozen ready for use, as well as chestnut purée in jars and cans, both of which are a great convenience to the cook.

However chestnuts are to be cooked, their shells must be cut before heating or they will explode. Take a sharp knife and cut an X on the flat side of each nut. To roast chestnuts, spread them in a shallow pan and roast in a 400°F/200°C/Gas Mark 5 oven for 25–30 minutes, or until chestnuts feel tender when pressed and the shells have curled where they were cut. Remove from the oven and, using a small sharp knife, remove shells and furry skin directly underneath. (Chestnuts are easiest to peel while still warm.) They are now ready to be puréed or treated in any way called for by the recipe.

To boil chestnuts, slash the shells as above and simmer for 15 minutes. Remove only one chestnut at a time and peel off the outer and inner skins. It is impossible to remove the inner skin if the nut has gone cold. Chestnuts can also be spread on a glass plate and microwaved for 5–6 minutes, stirring several times. Stand for 5 minutes and keep warm while peeling.

Green Gazpacho

This variation on the Spanish classic is lively and refreshing. Serve it
well-chilled on the hottest days or as a starter to a hearty meal. Lightly salted
bread sticks are the perfect accompaniment.

INGREDIENTS

2 slices day-old white bread, crusts removed

1 stalk celery, including leaves, chopped

6 tomatillos, husked and chopped

1 small green bell pepper (capsicum), seeded,
deribbed and cut up

2 large or 6 small pickling cucumbers, peeled
and cut up

1 fresh jalapeño chili, stemmed, seeded
(optional) and cut up

3 cloves garlic, crushed

1 teaspoon salt

Juice of 1 lime

3 tablespoons coarsely chopped cilantro (fresh
coriander/Chinese parsley) leaves

2 cups/16 fl oz/500 ml vegetable stock or water

MAYONNAISE

2 egg yolks

2 tablespoons tarragon vinegar

1½ teaspoons salt

½ teaspoon freshly ground pepper

⅔ cup/5 fl oz/160 ml olive oil

Fresh chives, chopped

½ small avocado, peeled and sliced

Preparation time about 30 minutes
Standing time 2 to 24 hours
Serves 4 to 6

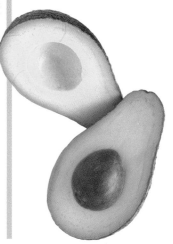

Soak bread in water to cover in a small bowl. Stand for 5 minutes, squeeze dry and set aside.

Combine celery with tomatillos, bell pepper, cucumbers, chili, bread, garlic, salt, lime juice and cilantro in a food processor fitted with a metal blade. Process to a fine purée. Add stock, working in batches, if necessary, and process until smooth. Set aside.

For mayonnaise, whisk egg yolks in a large bowl with vinegar, salt and pepper. Gradually add olive oil, drop by drop, whisking until an emulsion forms. As the mixture begins to thicken, you can add the oil more quickly. (If mayonnaise becomes too thick or starts to separate, add 1 tablespoon water and whisk vigorously.)

Once all the oil is added and the mayonnaise is thick, start adding the vegetable purée, ¼ cup/2 fl oz/60 ml at a time, whisking constantly, until thoroughly blended. Adjust seasoning and chill for 2–24 hours.

Ladle soup into chilled bowls. Sprinkle with chives and top each bowl with a slice of avocado.

A Classic Gazpacho

Do not use a food processor to make this soup or the bright color will be lost. Coarsely chop 6 full-flavored tomatoes and pass through a food mill fitted with a medium disk over a large bowl. Add about 8 oz/250 g peeled and finely chopped cucumber with 4 oz/125 g finely chopped celery, 4 oz/125 g seeded and finely chopped green bell pepper, 3 oz/90 g peeled and finely diced carrot, 3 oz/90 g peeled and finely chopped white onion, 3 tablespoons chopped parsley, 1 tablespoon extra-virgin olive oil, 2 teaspoons sherry wine vinegar, 1 teaspoon salt, or to taste, 3 cloves garlic, minced, 2 teaspoons dried oregano, 1 teaspoon sugar and 1 teaspoon freshly cracked pepper. Stir well. Transfer to a non-aluminum container and refrigerate, covered, overnight.

Pass mixture through a food mill fitted with a fine disk, or press through a sieve using the back of a spoon to extract as much liquid as possible. Adjust seasoning, cover and chill until serving time.

Ladle into chilled bowls and serve at once. Sprinkle with chopped basil, parsley or chives and top each bowl with a spoonful of sour cream or yogurt.

Serves 4.

Cream of Artichoke Soup

In this smooth, mellow soup, only the tender hearts of the artichokes are used. Armagnac adds a touch of luxury, but Cognac or any good-quality brandy will do just as well.

INGREDIENTS

6 medium-size artichokes

⅓ cup/2½ fl oz/80 ml olive oil

1 onion, coarsely chopped

3 stalks celery, coarsely chopped

1 large russet potato, peeled and coarsely chopped

6 cups/48 fl oz/1.5 l vegetable stock or water

2 oz/60 g hazelnuts

2 teaspoons salt, or to taste

1 teaspoon ground white pepper

2 cups/16 fl oz/500 ml heavy (double) cream

⅓ cup/2½ fl oz/80 ml Armagnac or good-quality brandy

Preparation time about 1 hour
Serves 6 to 8

Working with 1 artichoke at a time, cut off top half. Trim off stem even with the bottom. Snap or cut off all the tough outer leaves until you reach the tender pale green leaves. Carefully spread the tender leaves open and, with a small spoon, remove the prickly choke, leaving the inner leaves intact. Cut each trimmed artichoke lengthwise into 8 sections.

Preheat oven to 400°F/200°C/Gas Mark 5.

Heat olive oil in a large saucepan over medium heat. Add onion and celery and cook for 8–10 minutes, or until golden brown. Add artichokes, potato and stock and bring to the boil. Reduce heat, cover and simmer for about 45 minutes, or until the soup is slightly thickened and the flavors have developed.

While soup is cooking, toast and skin hazelnuts: spread nuts in a single layer on a baking sheet and toast in the oven for 5 minutes. Spread warm nuts on a kitchen towel, cover with another kitchen towel and rub gently against the nuts to remove as much of the skin as possible. Let cool. Chop nuts coarsely and set aside.

Working in batches, transfer soup to a blender or food processor fitted with a metal blade. Process on high speed for about 1 minute, or until smooth and creamy. Strain puréed soup through a fine-mesh sieve into a clean saucepan to remove any fibers. Add salt, pepper, cream and Armagnac, mix well and bring to a simmer, stirring, over medium heat.

Ladle soup into warmed bowls and sprinkle with chopped hazelnuts. Serve immediately.

Poached Eggs in Roasted Tomato Soup

This substantial Mexican meal, known as "drowned eggs", is served either as a good breakfast dish or for lunch with crusty bread and a salad. Be sure to roast the tomatoes until they are evenly charred for a lovely smoky flavor.

INGREDIENTS

4 tomatoes

4 cups/32 fl oz/1 l vegetable stock or water

2 tablespoons olive oil

1 yellow onion, thinly sliced

3 cloves garlic, minced

2 fresh serrano chilies

1 teaspoon salt

½ teaspoon freshly ground black pepper

8 eggs

1 oz/30 g Cotija, Romano or Parmesan cheese, grated

4 large flour tortillas, heated

Cooking time about 30 minutes
Serves 4

Broil tomatoes in a shallow pan 4–6 in/10–15 cm from the heat source, turning occasionally, for 10–12 minutes, or until charred all over. Remove and allow to cool slightly.

Cut out cores and process tomatoes in a food processor with 1 cup/8 fl oz/250 ml of the vegetable stock until smooth. Set aside.

Heat oil in a wide, heavy pan. Cook onion over medium heat for about 5 minutes, or until translucent. Add garlic and whole chilies and cook for 1 minute longer. Add tomato purée and remaining stock, season to taste and bring to the boil. Reduce heat and simmer, uncovered, for 10 minutes, or until flavors have blended.

Crack eggs, one at a time, into a cup and carefully slide them into the simmering soup. Baste tops with spoonfuls of hot soup for 4–6 minutes, or until whites are set but yolks are still soft.

Using a slotted spoon, carefully lift out eggs, placing 2 in each warmed soup bowl. Ladle soup over eggs and top with grated cheese. Serve immediately with warmed flour tortillas.

Oven-Dried Tomatoes

STEP 1

Halving Tomatoes

Plum (Roma) tomatoes are best for drying. Cut in half, lengthwise, from top to bottom and sprinkle with a little sea salt. Arrange, cut-side-down, on wire oven racks.

STEP 2

Drying Tomatoes

Place racks of tomato halves in the slowest possible oven with the fan on. The tomatoes will take from 4 to 12 hours to dry. Check on them from time to time to make sure they don't become leathery.

STEP 3

Storing Oven-Dried Tomatoes

Pack dried tomatoes into jars and cover with good-quality olive oil. Use, drained, as a garnish for soups or tossed through salads. Use the tomato-flavored oil in salad dressings to give them a lift.

Tuscan Vegetable Soup

The addition of a grain imparts body and rich flavor to this hearty country soup. Spelt, an old variety of wheat known in Tuscany as *farro*, is highly prized for its nuttiness and crunch. Look for it in well-stocked Italian food stores or health-food outlets.

INGREDIENTS

7 oz/220 g spelt, barley or long-grain white rice

4–5 cups/32–40 fl oz/1–1.25 l water

2 broccoli stalks

1 small leek, white part only

1 small stalk celery

1 large carrot, peeled

Olive oil

4 oz/125 g yellow onion, chopped

9 oz/280 g plum (Roma) tomatoes, peeled, seeded and chopped (fresh or canned)

2½ oz/80 g white turnip, peeled and thinly sliced

5 cups/40 fl oz/1.25 l vegetable stock

3½ oz/100 g beans, sliced on the diagonal

1 small zucchini (courgette), cut in half lengthways then thinly sliced crosswise

Salt and freshly ground pepper

Freshly grated Parmesan cheese

Preparation time about 20 minutes
Standing time 1 hour
Cooking time 1 to 1¼ hours
Serves 4

Soak grain in water to cover for 1 hour. Cut broccoli, leek, celery and carrot into ¼-in/6 mm-thick slices; set aside.

Heat 1 tablespoon oil in a large saucepan over low heat and cook onion for about 5 minutes, or until translucent. Add tomatoes and cook for 2 minutes. Drain grain and add to onion mixture along with sliced vegetables. Cook, stirring, for 3 minutes.

Add stock and 1 cup/8 fl oz/250 ml water and bring to the boil. Reduce heat and simmer, covered, for 15 minutes.

Add beans and zucchini and continue to simmer, stirring occasionally, for 35–40 minutes, or until vegetables are soft, but still hold their shape. If soup becomes too thick, stir in extra water. Season to taste.

Ladle soup into warmed bowls, pour a drizzle of olive oil over the top of each and sprinkle with cheese. Serve immediately.

STEP 1

Trimming Leeks

Trim off the root end of the leek and most of the green top.
Using a short, sharp chef's knife, cut the leek in half,
lengthways, from top to bottom.

STEP 2

Cleaning Leeks

Hold each leek half under running water. Hold the leaves apart
so the water can penetrate and rinse away any dirt that is
trapped between the layers. Dry thoroughly.

Glossary

The following glossary provides advice on selecting, purchasing
and storing some of the vegetables used in this book. See pages
13, 15 and 16 for photographs and information on grains and legumes.

squash

ARTICHOKES

Native to the Mediterranean, prickly artichokes look like tall thistles. The fleshy base of the inner leaves
and the bottom of the bud are tender when cooked; the remainder, including the rest of the leaf and the
fuzzy interior choke, are discarded. Fresh artichokes are sold all year in various sizes. Select compact,
heavy globes with tightly closed leaves; store in a plastic bag, refrigerated, for up to 4 days.

ASPARAGUS

These tender stalks are prized for their delicate flavor and marvelous green hue, sometimes tinged with
purple at the cap (white asparagus, a delicacy, is much less common). Crisp, straight, firm stalks with
tight buds are best. Store wrapped in damp paper towels in a plastic bag, refrigerated, for up to 4 days.

AVOCADOS

Two main varieties of tropical avocado are common: buttery Hass, with a green-black, rough skin, and
blander Fuerte, with a thin, smooth skin. Ripe avocados yield to gentle thumb pressure. Choose firm-ripe
unblemished avocados and store in the refrigerator for several days. Ripen at warm room temperature or,
more quickly, in a paper bag.

BEANS

The familiar green beans and yellow wax beans are the edible immature pods of the bean plant, a legume. Another variety is the small delicate French bean, or haricot vert. Fresh beans are firm and smooth, without bruising or spotting; avoid those that are leathery or bulging with seeds. Store in a loosely closed plastic bag, chilled, for up to 4 days.

BEETS

No part of a beet goes to waste; both the bulbous root and the leafy, deep-green tops are edible. The dense, deep-red flesh is enclosed by a dark, papery skin that is peeled before eating; other varieties are golden yellow or creamy white. Store in a plastic bag, refrigerated (with root intact, but greens trimmed to 1 in/2.5 cm), for up to 1 month; greens will keep for 3 to 5 days.

BROCCOLI

Choose firm stalks and closed heads with deep color and no yellow areas. Store, refrigerated, in a plastic bag for up to 4 days.

BRUSSELS SPROUTS

The best are small with tight heads and no odor. They are most flavorful if purchased on the stalk; trim off just before cooking. Store in a plastic bag, refrigerated, for up to 2 days.

CABBAGE

A large and diverse family. Choose a cabbage with a firm, heavy head, unblemished leaves and a moist core. Store in a plastic bag, refrigerated, for up to 2 weeks.

beets

CHICORY AND ENDIVE

The confusing term chicory refers to several distinctive greens. Belgian endive—also called chicory—is a compact shoot with tightly furled light-green or yellow-tipped white leaves. Ruffle-edged curly endive, or frisée—often called chicory—and smooth-edged escarole are slightly bitter greens that add depth of flavor and a crunchy texture to salads, but taste mild when cooked. Select Belgian endive with compact, unblemished heads; curly endive and escarole should look fresh and lively. Store in a plastic bag, refrigerated, for up to 3 days.

EGGPLANT

Most forms have purple skins (although some have white). Cooked eggplant is mild-flavored, with tender, creamy flesh. Look for plump, glossy eggplants that are heavy for their size with taut skin free of bruises or scratches. Store, refrigerated, in a plastic bag for up to 2 days.

FENNEL

Crisp and juicy, like celery, fennel has a flavor reminiscent of licorice. Tubular stalks and feathery leaves attach to a bulbous base, which should be free of cracks or brown spots. Store, refrigerated, in a plastic bag for up to 4 days.

GARLIC

A head, or bulb, of garlic is formed of numerous small cloves, all wrapped in a papery outer skin. Sharp when raw, the taste of garlic becomes delicate when cooked. Bulbs should be plump and firm; store in a cool, dark, dry spot.

eggplant

JÍCAMA

This vegetable has crisp white flesh. Choose jícamas that are firm and heavy. Store whole, refrigerated, for up to 3 weeks; once cut, wrap in plastic wrap (film) and chill for up to 1 week.

KOHLRABI

An unusual vegetable that is like its cabbage relatives in flavor and texture, but not appearance. The leaves are like spinach, but are often trimmed away. Fresh bulbs are sold from spring through fall. Choose those smaller than 3 in (7.5 cm); avoid any with cracks. Store, chilled, in a plastic bag for up to 1 week.

kohlrabi

LEEKS

Buy small-to-medium, healthy-looking leeks with crisp green leaves; large ones more than 1 in (2.5 cm) in diameter tend to be tough. Store in a plastic bag, refrigerated, for up to 5 days. Rinse leeks carefully, separating the leaves, as dirt gets trapped between them.

MUSHROOMS

There are numerous varieties, colors and sizes of fungi. Common or button mushrooms are white, cream or brown, with a mild flavor. Shiitakes are an Asian variety with floppy, meaty dark-brown caps and tough, thin stems that are usually trimmed off and discarded. Wild Italian porcini (cèpes, in French) are fragrant, earthy and expensive, with round caps and thick stems. Select firm, fresh, plump mushrooms that aren't bruised or slimy. Store in the refrigerator, lightly wrapped in paper towels or in a paper bag, never in plastic. Use quickly.

ONIONS

Onios can be white, yellow or reddish-purple. Green (spring) onions are immature, with more green stalk than white bulb. Shallots grow in clumps of small cloves like garlic, and have papery skins. Tiny chives have fine hollow stalks and no bulb. Store onions and shallots in a cool, dark, dry place for up to 2 weeks. Refrigerate green onions in a plastic bag and store chives as you would an herb (use as soon as possible).

PEAS

Only the seeds of the round, sweet English pea are eaten. Thin, crisp snow peas and plump sugar snap peas (mangetout) are eaten pod and all. All three varieties are available almost all year, both fresh and frozen. Choose crisp pods with bright green color and store, chilled, in a plastic bag for 2 to 3 days.

leeks

RUTABAGAS

Part turnip, part cabbage, the yellow rutabaga has firm yellow flesh and a tan, green or purple skin. The sweetest are no more than 3 to 4 in (7.5 to 10 cm) in diameter and should be firm and heavy for their size. Store in a plastic bag in the refrigerator for up to 1 month.

SQUASH

Soft-skinned, slender green and yellow zucchini, yellow crookneck squashes and pattypan squashes are classified as "summer" squash, although many are sold year-round. They can all be used interchangeably. Choose heavy, well-shaped squash without cracks or bruises. They will keep for up to 4 days in the refrigerator. Winter squash are harvested after the skin has hardened. Buy winter squash that are heavy for their size, with hard skins. Whole squash will keep for several months in a cool, dry place; wrap cut pieces and store, refrigerated, for 3 to 4 days.

SWEET POTATOES

The golden sweet potato and orange yam are neither potato nor yam but tuberous roots from the morning glory family (true yams are another vegetable entirely and very rare). Sweet potatoes are sweet and creamy when baked or boiled. Choose sweet potatoes with firm, smooth skins. Store in a cool, dark place and use within 1 week.

SWISS CHARD

A beet relative, this leafy vegetable has crinkly green leaves and either a white or scarlet stem (both types are interchangeable). Select chard with crisp, unblemished leaves. Wash in cold water, pat dry and store in a plastic bag lined with a paper towel, refrigerated, for up to 3 days.

water chestnuts

WATER CHESTNUTS

Crisp white tubers with dark brown skins, they stay crunchy, sweet and fresh-tasting even when cooked. Good in everything from stir-fries to soups to stuffings. Buy fresh water chestnuts in specialty markets; canned peeled water chestnuts, whole or sliced, are available from supermarkets and Asian markets.

Index

Entries in *italics* indicate illustrations and photos.

ACKNOWLEDGMENTS

Weldon Owen would like to thank the following people: Sarah Anderson, Lisa Boehm, Trudie Craig, Janine Flew, Peta Gorman, Michael Hann, Puddingburn Publishing Services (index)
Photography Ad-Libitum/Stuart Bowey, John Callanan, Kevin Candland, Rowan Fotheringham, John Hollingshead, Peter Johnson, Joyce Oudkerk Pool, Penina, Alejandro Pradera, Chris Shorten
Styling Janice Baker, Penny Farrell, Kay Francis, Stephanie Greenleigh, Jane Hann, Susan Massey, Pouké, Vicki Roberts-Russell